JAMES A. GARFIELD
1831 - 1881

CHESTER A. ARTHUR
1830 - 1886

Chronology—Documents—Bibliographical Aids

Edited by
Howard B. Furer

Series Editor
Howard F. Bremer

1970
OCEANA PUBLICATIONS, INC.
Dobbs Ferry, New York

TABLE OF CONTENTS

BIBLIOGRAPHICAL AIDS

EDITOR'S FOREWORD

Every effort has been made to cite the most accurate dates possible in the chronologies of James A. Garfield and Chester A. Arthur. No difficulties were experienced in the case of Garfield as there were copious amounts of material from which to draw. In Arthur's chronology, however, a number of conflicting dates were encountered. This was due to the fact that most of the material had to be taken from newspapers and the papers of political associates and opponents, as no real collection of personal papers exists. Therefore, when conflict arose the most plausible date was selected.

This work is intended as a starting point for those students interested in pursuing further the life and work of two lesser known, but interesting Presidents. Time has brought both Garfield and Arthur an obscurity in strange contrast to their significant part in American history. Both really played important roles in the development of the nation, and both led remarkably similar lives.

While the editor has tried to remain objective in his approach, some judgments on the significance of events and men have been made. It is hoped that they are reasoned judgments. The documents in this volume are taken from: James D. Richardson, ed., *Messages and Papers of the Presidents*. Vol. *X*, Washington, 1897.

CHRONOLOGY

YOUTH AND EARLY CAREER

1831

November 19   Born: Cleveland, Ohio as James Abram Garfield. Father: Abram. Mother: Eliza Ballou.

1834

March   Father, Abram, died leaving four small children of whom James was the youngest.

1835

Attended school in a log hut, where he learned to read. At age ten, James was accustomed to manual labor, helping out his mother's meager income by work at home or on the farms of neighbors. During the winter months he attended the district school, and by the age of fourteen had a fair knowledge of arithmetic and grammar. He excelled in American history.

1848

August 16   Having left home at the age of seventeen, Garfield determined to become a sailor. He took a job as part of the crew of the canal boat, *Evening Star* which was taking a load of copper ore destined for Pittsburgh.

August 26   Reached Pittsburgh. It was the first time Garfield had been as much as twenty miles from home. The boat was loaded with coal for the return trip, and Garfield was promoted to bowman at the salary of fourteen dollars a month.

October 3   Fell ill with fever, and returned to his mother's cabin to be nursed back to health. His canal experience came to an abrupt conclusion.

1849

April   Attended the Geauga Seminary at Chester, Ohio during the winter of 1849-50. During the vacations, Garfield learned

1

and practiced the trade of carpenter, helped at the harvest, and did anything and everything to earn money to pay for his schooling. Finished his studies at Geauga in the summer of 1851.

November 10 Began teaching school in a district not far from his boyhood home. He was eighteen years old and his classroom often witnessed a struggle for mastery between the older boys and the young teacher. His salary was thirteen dollars a month. Early in March, the short term of school in District number Two came to a close, and Garfield was unemployed until the following November when school resumed.

1850
March 4 Was converted under the instructions of a Disciples of Christ preacher; was baptised and received into that denomination. To Garfield, conversion was a great emotional experience, and he wrote that he "was buried with Christ in Baptism and arose to walk in newness of life."

1851
October 2 Entered the Western Reserve Eclectic Institute at Hiram, Ohio. This academy was the principal educational institution of his church. In addition to his studies, Garfield was engaged as a teacher in the elementary branches, and was no longer compelled to interrupt his residence to teach in some district school.

1854
June 15 Graduated from Hiram Eclectic Institute. During his last year at the Institute, Garfield decided to complete his college education in some new environment. He wrote to various colleges, including Yale, Brown and Williams. He chose Williams and arrived in Williamstown early in July, 1854.

September 1 Admitted to the Junior class at Williams and began two years at the college upon which Garfield always looked back with gratitude and affection. Graduated in August, 1856 standing second in a class of forty-five. In the commencement exercises, he delivered the "Metaphysical Oration."

1856
October 4 Returned to Ohio, and resumed his duties as a teacher of Latin and Greek at Hiram Institute. During the next five

years, Garfield, the preacher and evangelist, preached the gospel of the Disciples of Christ somewhere every Sunday.

November 4 Cast his vote for John C. Fremont, the Republican candidate for President. During the campaign, he had engaged in debates which had helped to swing the vote of Northern Ohio to Fremont.

1857

May 26 At the age of twenty-six, he was chosen by the Trustees of Hiram Institute to be its President. The entire faculty at that time, consisted of five instructors.

1858

November 11 At the home of Zeb Rudolph in Hiram, Garfield was married to Lucretia Rudolph, whom he had met and fell in love with, several years earlier at the Institute.

December 18-23 Debated John Denton, a well educated Englishman, on the question of religious orthodoxy versus natural law and spontaneous generation. As a result of this debate, Garfield became the outstanding defender of religion against "infidelity," and gained a host of friends setting the stage for his first step in political advancement. He followed up his initial success with a series of lectures in various towns on the subject, "Geology and Religion," during the winter of 1858-59.

1859

June 12 Advised by Harmon Austin of Ravenna, Ohio, a member of the Board of Trustees at Hiram, to run for the Ohio State Legislature. Garfield agreed.

August 26 Attended Republican State Convention in Cleveland, where he was selected by the delegates to run for the State Senate seat representing Summit and Portage Counties.

October 16-18 John Brown, a fanatical abolitionist from Kansas, seized the Federal arsenal and armory at Harper's Ferry, Virginia. After two days of battle, Brown and his surviving followers were taken prisoner by a force of U.S. Marines commanded by Colonel Robert E. Lee.

November 5 Elected to the Ohio State Senate by a commanding majority of more than 1400 votes in a total of nine thousand. Garfield had campaigned on an anti-slavery plank, made more than thirty speeches, and had laid deep foundations for his political career.

1860

January 10　Attended inaugural ceremonies at Columbus, Ohio of Governor-Elect William Dennison.

January 15　Sworn into his seat in the Ohio State Senate. Garfield soon became friends with James Monroe, a professor at Oberlin College, and Jacob D. Cox. The three men became inseparable and were the leaders of the more radical element among the Republicans.

May 3　The National Democratic convention at Charleston, South Carolina adjourned having failed to agree on a nominee after 57 ballots.

June 18　The Northern Democrats reassembled at Baltimore and nominated Stephen A. Douglas of Illinois for President, and Herschel V. Johnson of Georgia for Vice-President.

June 28　At Baltimore, the Southern Democrats nominated John C. Breckinridge of Kentucky for President and Joseph Lane of Oregon for Vice-President. The Republicans, meeting in Chicago, on May 16, had nominated Abraham Lincoln of Illinois for President and Hannibal Hamlin of Maine for Vice-President. Garfield, wholeheartedly endorsed the Republican ticket, and throughout the entire campaign devoted himself to the topic of unity. He attacked Douglas, and stated that the idea of popular sovereignty opened up more problems than it settled.

November 6　Cast his vote for Lincoln and Hamlin, and in the evening went to Ravenna to receive the returns, which gave Lincoln and the Republicans a great victory. Garfield was overjoyed, and stated that he was happy that the questions of slavery and union had been met squarely.

December 20　South Carolina seceded from the Union. She was followed, during the next two months, by ten other states, which ultimately formed the Confederate States of America on February 8, 1861.

1861

January 7 Returned to Columbus for the annual meeting of the Ohio Legislature. He was greatly disturbed by the secession of the Southern states.

January 15 In a letter to Burke Hinsdale, Garfield stated that peaceable dissolution of the Union was impossible. He believed that the Northern states should arm themselves to defend the Federal Government.

March 4 Abraham Lincoln was inaugurated as the sixteenth President of the United States. He delivered a firm, but conciliatory address concerning the seceded Southern States. Garfield was disappointed in Lincoln's first inaugural address feeling that the President was unequal to the heroic demands of the hour. Garfield was never an admirer of Lincoln, and in the years to come, he was one of Lincoln's most severe critics on several important issues.

April 12 The Civil War began, as Confederate artillery opened fire on Ft. Sumter, located in the harbor of Charleston, South Carolina.

April 13 Garfield and Cox met with Governor Dennison, and the the three men decided to arm and equip the militia, and to ask the legislature for authority to borrow half a million dollars for the purpose. This agreement was reached a full day before Ohio received word of what had happened at Ft. Sumter.

April 14 When word reached Garfield concerning the action at Sumter, he expressed delight at the opening of hostilities. He stated that war was just what was needed to shake the government and people from their lethargy, and to prevent the nation from drifting into disunion.

April 15 Opposed, in the Ohio Senate, the proposed "Corwin Amendment," sponsored by Thomas Corwin of Ohio, which would have reassured the South by removing slavery in the states from the reach of national action. Nevertheless, the "Corwin Amendment" was approved by the Ohio Legislature. At the same time, however, Garfield succeeded in pushing through the Legislature his own "Million Bill," providing for a state loan for arms and equipment for the militia.

June 1   Became an active candidate for the Colonelcy of one of the Ohio regiments, but lost this office in a bitter contest to Erastus B. Tyler of Ravenna.

June 5   Governor Dennison offered Garfield the position of Lieutenant Colonel of one of the new Ohio regiments. Garfield decided not to enter the army at this time.

August 14   Accepted the post which in June he had refused. Sent a telegram to Governor Dennison informing him that he was now ready to take up "the call of war." Garfield reported three days later to the Forty-Second Regiment Ohio Volunteers.

CIVIL WAR

August 28   Was promoted by Governor Dennison to the rank of Colonel in command of the Forty-Second Ohio.

November 30 After having recruited his regiment in Hiram and the surrounding towns, Garfield found himself in command of a full regiment of a thousand men.

December 14 Summoned to active duty. Garfield and the Forty-Second Ohio reported to General Don C. Buell in Louisville, Kentucky. Was given command of a brigade, and assigned the difficult task of driving the Confederate general Humphrey Marshall from eastern Kentucky.

1862

January 10   Defeated Marshall and the Confederate forces at the battle of Middle Creek, Kentucky. This battle was the only one in which Garfield was destined to command. In recognition of his services, and through the lobbying of his Ohio friends in Washington, Garfield was promoted to the rank of Brigadier General by President Lincoln.

March 14   Led a small expedition against General Marshall who had retired to Pound Gap on the Virginia border. Again defeated the Confederate forces in a blinding snow storm. When he returned to his headquarters at Louisville, he was ordered to turn over his command to Colonel Jonathan Cranor, and to join Buell, whose army was then on its way to join

Grant on the banks of the Tennessee River for the proposed advance on Corinth, Mississippi.

April 4   Joined Buell at a point thirty miles south of Columbia, Tennessee, and was assigned to the command of the Twentieth Brigade made up of two Ohio regiments, one from Michigan, and one from Indiana. Garfield's division commander was Major General T. J. Wood.

April 6   The battle of Shiloh began. Garfield's troops marched toward Shiloh but did not reach the battlefield until the next morning.

April 7   Reached Shiloh in time to take part in the second day's fight which consisted mainly of minor contests with the Confederates who were now falling back.

April 18-   Was engaged in all the operations in front of Corinth, which
May 31   finally fell to Major General Henry Halleck.

June 1-12   Rebuilt the bridges on the Memphis and Charleston Railroad, and exhibited noticeable engineering skill in repairing the fortifications of Huntsville.

June 15   Made president of a court-martial board which was to try several officers under the command of General O. M. Mitchell for crimes against civilian populations in the South. This unpleasant duty occupied the last six weeks of Garfield's service in Buell's army. Garfield's own vote in the court-martial cases was not recorded.

June 25   Wrote to his political manager, Harmon Austin, that he would like to enter Congress. Early in May, his Hiram friends had written to him explaining that the political situation was favorable and that if he allowed his name to be brought up before the Republican convention, he would be almost certain of an election to Congress.

July 30   Was granted a leave of absence on account of ill health, and returned to Hiram, where he lay ill for two months.

August 12   Declared that he was an active candidate for the Ohio Nineteenth Congressional District seat. However, Garfield stated that he would not resign his commission in the army unless his duties in the new Congress were imperative.

September 2 The Ohio Republican Convention met at Garrettsville. Garfield was the only one of five candidates who was not present in person at the convention. Nevertheless, on the eighth ballot, Garfield was nominated over incumbent Congressman John Hutchins by a vote of 78 to 71. Garfield's friends at the convention worked extremely hard to get the nomination for their man.

September 19 Arrived in Washington, D.C., where as a guest of Secretary of the Treasury Salmon P. Chase, Garfield met Congressmen, politicans, contractors, and ambitious soldiers, who were all seeking opportunities for personal advancement. Garfield, too, was soon numbered among their group.

September 21 Lincoln signed the preliminary proclamation of emancipation. Garfield was immensely pleased with the emancipation proclamation, which he prophesied would bring strength to Lincoln in all parts of the country. Garfield, however, disapproved of Lincoln's suggestion of gradual emancipation.

September 25 Assigned to court-martial duty in Washington.

October 4 Elected to Congress from the Nineteenth Congressional District. Garfield defeated his Democratic opponent by a vote of almost two to one.

October 8 Called on Secretary of War Edwin M. Stanton in an attempt to obtain a separate command in the field. It was suggested by Garfield's friend, Secretary Chase, that Garfield be sent with 20,000 men to occupy confiscated rebel plantations in Florida. Stanton seemed to agree, subject to General Halleck's approval which was not obtained. Garfield, who had never been fond of "West Point men" was now strengthened in his conviction that high military rank should be earned on the battlefield, not in the classroom, or in the offices of politicians.

November 21 Appointed to the court-martial board which was to try Major-General Fitz-John Porter on the serious charges of disobedience of orders, insubordination, and treachery at the second battle of Bull Run.

November 27- The court-martial board in the Fitz-John Porter case met
January 10   almost continuously.

1863

January 21   Porter was found guilty, cashiered, and forever disqualified
                  from holding any office of profit or trust under the govern-
                  ment of the United States. Garfield voted in favor of convic-
                  tion, and even after a new trial in 1878 completely exoner-
                  ated Porter, he continued to defend the court-martial of 1862.
                  In 1886, President Cleveland signed an act by which Porter
                  was reappointed to the army with the rank of Colonel,
                  retroactive from May 14, 1861. As a party chieftan, during
                  his later career, Garfield found it necessary to defend the
                  sentence of the court.

January 25   Returned to duty, after a brief visit at Hiram. Garfield re-
                  ported to Murfreesboro, Tennessee, the headquarters of
                  General W.S. Rosecrans, in command of the Army of the
                  Cumberland. The relations between the two men were, for
                  the next nine months, to be peculiarly intimate. A great
                  friendship was established, which would one day change to
                  intense hatred.

February 14   Rosecrans appointed Garfield his chief of staff, with respon-
                  sibilities beyond those usually given to this office. In this
                  position, Garfield's influence on the campaign in middle
                  Tennessee was most important.

June 24   Before the battle of Chickamauga, General Rosecrans asked
                  the written opinion of seventeen of his generals on the
                  advisability of an immediate advance. While all the others
                  opposed this action, Garfield advised it, and his arguments
                  were so convincing that Rosecrans decided to press forward
                  with his plan. The campaign was a complete success, and by
                  early July, the Union army was in control of the entire
                  region north of the Tennessee River having captured the
                  Confederate base at Tullahoma.

July 27   Wrote a letter to Secretary Chase criticising Rosecrans for
                  not following the Confederates after the victory at Tullahoma.
                  Garfield maintained that he had advised Rosecrans to do
                  so, but that his advice had not been heeded, thus allowing
                  the Confederate army to escape. This letter, unknown to

Rosecrans at the time, was one of the major reasons for the bitter hatred that developed between the two men.

August 16-22 As the battle of Chattanooga was about to begin, Garfield was confined to his tent by illness for ten days, and was unable to take an active part in the opening stages of the campaign.

September 19 Wrote out all the orders for the field commanders at the battle of Chickamauga. However, Rosecrans and Garfield, commanding the troops on the right, were defeated by the Confederates. Garfield volunteered to take the news of the defeat on the right to General George H. Thomas, who held the left of the line. Garfield's dangerous ride became a legend. For this action, he was promoted to the rank of Major General.

September 30 Generals Garfield, T.J. Wood, and Emerson Opdyke reported to Charles A. Dana, Secretary of War Stanton's personal emissary, that the Army of the Cumberland had lost confidence in Rosecrans. They suggested that Thomas replace him as the new commander.

October 10 Desirous of returning to Washington to take up his duties as a Congressman, Garfield asked to be relieved from his duties as Chief of Staff. Rosecrans complied with Garfield's wishes.

October 11 His first son, Harry Augustus Garfield, was born at Hiram.

October 15 As a special messenger from Rosecrans, bearing the report of the Chattanooga-Chickamauga campaign and other dispatches, Garfield left Tennessee for Washington.

October 21 Met with Secretary Stanton in Louisville, Kentucky, and related his crticisms of Rosecrans' handling of the campaigns in Tennessee. Rosecrans was removed shortly thereafter. Rosecrans did not learn of Garfield's part in his dismissal until 1874, when Charles Dana, in an article written for the *New York Sun,* made the charges against Rosecrans public, and placed the blame for Rosecrans' removal on Garfield.

December 5 Resigned his commission in the army at the request of

President Lincoln after having been assured that his place in the army would be kept open whenever he decided to return.

December 7   Took his seat in the Thirty-Eighth Congress. Was assigned to the Military Committee, then the most important in Congress.

CONGRESSIONAL CAREER
1864

January 28   Delivered his first important speech in the House on the confiscation of rebel property, and in support of a bill that had been introduced by J. F. Wilson of Iowa which was a direct challenge to the doctrines of moderate Reconstruction as proposed by Lincoln. Garfield had placed himself on the extreme left and in opposition to the President.

February 5   Garfield cast his vote in the House in favor of Wilson's confiscation bill. The Senate, however, took no action, and this ended all serious attempts to legislate further upon the confiscation of rebel property as a punishment for treason.

February 8   Placed in charge of the first military bill of the Thirty Eighth Session of Congress. Garfield was primarily responsible for the drafting of this piece of legislation which reduced the number of reasons for exemption from the army. The House passed the Garfield Bill on February 14, but the Senate delayed action. The debate over the Garfield Bill raged for several months. Lincoln, himself, joined in the fight for passage saying that without more soldiers the war could not be won.

February 22   Many Republicans in Congress had become disenchanted with Lincoln, and as 1864 was a Presidential election year, several other candidates were proposed for the Republican nomination. The "Pomeroy Circular" appeared placing Salmon P. Chase in active candidacy. Garfield was placed in a difficult position, for though he was a good friend of Chase, he believed the people wanted the reelection of Lincoln.

April 8   In a speech full of burning invective, Garfield debated Congressman Alexander Long of Cincinnati who had risen in the House and urged immediate recognition of the Confederacy if the continuance of the war would lead to confiscation and social revolution. Garfield argued for victory and union. His powerful oratory attracted the attention of the nation.

April 30   Garfield made no secret of his preference for Chase as the Republican Presidential nominee, but was certain that Lincoln would be renominated, and then defeated by a Democrat in November.

May 31   Did not attend the Cleveland, Ohio convention of Radical Republicans which nominated John C. Fremont for the Presidency, even though the criticisms of Lincoln in the Radical platform were the very ones which he himself was making.

June 7   Attended, with reluctance, the Baltimore convention of the Union Republican Party which unanimously nominated Lincoln for the Presidency, and Andrew Johnson of Tennessee for Vice President.

June 13   Took a leading part in introducing a resolution in the House to the effect that no Southern state reorganized by Lincoln's plan of Reconstruction should be eligible to cast its votes for President or Vice President without the previous consent of both houses of Congress. The resolution was defeated.

June 25   Delivered one of the most powerful and effective speeches of his career in support of Lincoln's policy—concerning the increased draft, and the reduction of the number of reasons for exemption from the army.

July 1   The Senate, at the very end of its sessions, passed the Garfield Bill of February 8, although Garfield was forced to accompany it with an unfortunate amendment that was to be a source of great injustice. By the Garfield Amendment, volunteers in Southern States might, by a legal fiction, be credited to the quota of some Northern State, thus reducing its own obligations under the draft. An unseemly scramble for soldiers ensued. Apart from this amendment, Garfield had made a fine record in support of the effective maintenance of a national army.

August 5   Accepted the Wade-Davis Manifesto proposed by Senators Benjamin Wade of Ohio and Representative Henry W. Davis of Maryland which castigated Lincoln for his pocket veto of a Congressional Reconstruction Plan (Wade-Davis Bill) in favor of his own Ten Per-Cent Plan of Reconstruction.

August 23   Garfield was charged with a part in the authorship of the Wade-Davis Manifesto because of his intimacy with Wade and Davis. When the Ohio Congressional Nominating Convention met in Warren, Ohio, Garfield was invited to appear before the meeting to explain the charges that had been made against him. Garfield appeared, denied having written the document, stated that he had not opposed the nomination of Lincoln at Baltimore, but disapproved of his policies, and said that unless he could be nominated with perfect freedom to express his views on public issues, he did not want the nomination. Moved by his courage, the convention renominated Garfield by acclamation.

August 29   The Democratic National Convention at Chicago nominated General George C. McClellan for President, and George H. Pendleton of Ohio for Vice President.

September 2   General William T. Sherman occupied Atlanta, Georgia.

September 21   Fremont withdrew from the election.

October 3   Was elected to Congress for the second time by a vote of 18,086 to 6,315. Garfield took an active part in the general campaign, making more than sixty speeches and invading Holmes County, Ohio, and other centers of Democratic strength.

November 8   Lincoln was reelected by 212-21 electoral votes, but with a popular majority of but 400,000 out of 4 million votes cast.

1865

January 18   Made a speech in the House attacking the policy of military imprisonments as both illegal and unnecessary. He firmly stated that civilians could not be placed in military prisons without due process of law.

January 20   Sworn into his seat in the Thirty-Ninth Congress. At his own request, Garfield was changed from the Committee on Military Affairs to the Committee on Ways and Means.

March 4   Attended Lincoln's Second Inaugural in Washington, and
                  although impressed with what the President said, he con-
                  tinued to favor Congressional policies toward reconstruction.

April 9   General Robert E. Lee surrendered to General Ulysses S.
                  Grant at Appomatox Courthouse in Virginia. For all
                  intents and purposes, the Civil War was over.

April 15   Learned of Lincoln's assassination in New York City where
                  he had gone on a business trip. He helped to calm a large
                  crowd who had gathered outside of the *New York World*
                  building (a Democratic newspaper), but he had no praise
                  for Lincoln in his short address.

May 29   President Andrew Johnson issued his own Reconstruction
                  Proclamation in which he committed himself to almost
                  exactly the same method of reconstruction that had al-
                  ready been begun by Lincoln. Garfield opposed the John-
                  son Plan just as he had opposed the Lincoln Plan.

July 4   Delivered an oration at Ravenna in which he boldly dis-
                  cussed the problem of Negro suffrage. Despite his own feeling
                  that it might be dangerous to extend the franchise to "the
                  great mass of ignorant and degraded blacks, so lately
                  slaves," Garfield stated that he had come to feel that the
                  ballot must be given to the Negro to permit his own protec-
                  tion against injustice. At the same time, he hinted at getting
                  the newly enfranchised Negro to vote for the Republican
                  party.

December 4   The Thirty-Ninth Congress reconvened, and refused to
                  endorse Johnson's reconstruction policies. Garfield voted
                  against all of Johnson's proposals, and was a member of the
                  Republican Caucus led by Thaddeus Stevens of Pennsyl-
                  vania, which resolved not to recognize any of the newly
                  reconstructed governments of the South. Also became friend-
                  ly with Roscoe Conkling of New York, and Rutherford B.
                  Hayes of Ohio whom he met for the first time.

December 9   Met with President Johnson to discuss Reconstruction
                  policies. No agreement was reached between the two men,
                  but Garfield came away with the impression that the
                  President would soon cooperate with the Radical Repub-
                  licans.

1866

February 1 Adopted a thorough going position of nationalism on the question of the "nature of the Union." To all Constitutional scruples as to Radical Reconstruction policy, Garfield opposed what seemed to him "the unanswerable proposition that this is a nation."

February 19 Johnson vetoed the first of the Congressional measures of Reconstruction, the Freedman's Bureau Bill which took the Negro problem from the states and placed it under national authority.

March 6 Presented before the Supreme Court of the United States his argument in the case of *ex parte Milligan.* This was the first and most important of Garfield's legal adventures. Garfield had studied law on his own at Hiram College, and under the easy regulations of that time had been admitted to the bar in 1858. The case originated in the arrest at Indianapolis (October 5, 1864) of L.P. Milligan, who with several associates was condemned by a military commission and sentenced to be hanged. The accusation was conspiracy to release "rebel" prisoners, and to cooperate with the Confederates. The execution was postponed pending an appeal to the United States Supreme Court. There the matter rested until 1866. Garfield acted as the defense attorney, and won an outstanding victory when the Court ruled that military tribunals are unconstitutional where civil courts are in operation.

April 9 Voted in favor of the Civil Rights Act (bestowing citizenship upon the Negro) over President Johnson's veto.

June 13 Voted in favor of the Fourteenth Amendment which guaranteed the suffrage to Negroes, abrogated the three-fifths clause of the Constitution, and provided a proportionate reduction in representation when a state denied suffrage. It was ratified by the states as of July 28, 1868.

July 16 Voted in favor of the Freedman's Bureau Bill (a temporary bureau to care for the Negroes and the abandoned lands of the South) over President Johnson's veto.

August 1 Announced his candidacy for reelection to Congress. Began a very vigorous campaign throughout his district.

September 1   Spoke at Warren, Ohio. Condemned the Democratic Party and President Johnson in a very effective piece of oratory. "Waving the Bloody Shirt" proved quite successful for him in this campaign.

November 6   Garfield won reelection to the House easily by a vote of 18,362 to 7,376. The Republicans won 66-2/3% of the seats, with the Radicals firmly in control.

1867

January 1   Asserted that he believed that the Southern states should adopt the Fourteenth Amendment or face an even harsher reconstruction policy.

January 20   Sworn into his seat in the Fortieth Congress. Garfield was restored to the Committee on Military Affairs and made its chairman.

February 8   Gave his assent to a bill which divided the South into military districts. This was the first step in the Congressional program of reconstruction.

March 2   Voted in favor of the First Reconstruction Act over President Johnson's veto. In fact, Garfield gave his assent to every Congressional bill adopted to complete the program of Reconstruction in the South. These included the Tenure of Office Act, the Command of the Army Act, the Supplementary Reconstruction Acts, and the Omnibus Act among others.

1868

January 17   Attacked General Winfield S. Hancock, commander of the Southern military district of Louisiana and Texas, for following a mild policy in carrying out the provisions of the Reconstruction acts. At the same time, Garfield introduced a bill to reduce the number of Major Generals in the Army. Since Hancock was the newest member on the list, he would be the first to go. The bill aroused a storm of protest both in Congress itself and among the public.

February 24   Though nominally a Radical Republican, Garfield could not be persuaded that President Johnson was guilty of high crimes and misdemeanors within the meaning of the Constitution, and voted against the proposed policy. When the

Covode Resolution of Impeachment passed the House, Garfield was among the small number of Republicans who were absent from their seats.

February 27   General Hancock, at his own request, was relieved of his command in the Fifth District. Garfield had won a complete victory although the so called "Hancock Bill" never came to a vote. After the removal of Hancock, Garfield became increasingly doubtful of the wisdom of Radical Republican Reconstruction policy.

May 15   Delivered a major address in the House on the subject of the currency in which he strongly urged the passage of a bill requiring the resumption of specie payments. Garfield had come out as early as 1865 as a "hard money" man, and continued in this position until his death. In 1866, he had opposed payment of the national debt in greenbacks, and the very arguments that he had used then, were later used by McKinley and the Republicans in the election of 1896. He opposed inflation, and stood alone on this position from out of all the representatives of the Mississippi Valley states.

May 20-21   Attended the Republican National Convention in Chicago where he cast his vote for Ulysses S. Grant and Schuyler Colfax of Indiana as his party's candidates in the 1868 presidential election.

July 9   At the Democratic National Convention in New York City, Horatio Seymour of New York and Francis P. Blair of Missouri were nominated for the Presidency and Vice Presidency respectively.

July 15   Had a sharp clash with Congressmen John A. Logan of Illinois and Benjamin F. Butler of Massachusetts on the question of a tax of ten percent on the interest of government bonds. Garfield opposed the tax saying it would be ruinous to the credit of the country, and that it would cost more to administer than it would yield in revenue.

July 23   Debated Thaddeus Stevens who opposed repayment of the bonds in coin. Garfield offered a plan for a prompt return to specie payments. It was given no serious consideration. Garfield's position on the money question was quite courageous since most of his party's leaders had already come out in favor of payment of the bonds in greenbacks. Nevertheless, he stuck to his convictions, and by 1869 his position was to emerge victorious.

November 3   Grant was elected President with an electoral vote of 214-80, but a popular majority of only 306,000 out of 5,715,000 votes. Garfield vigorously supported Grant, and campaigned throughout Ohio for him. Garfield easily won his reelection attempt and prepared for his fourth term in Congress.

1869

January 16   Bought a home in Washington for a sum of $10,000. The Garfields, when not in Washington continued to make their home in Hiram, where the Congressman took an active interest in the old college of which he was now a trustee.

January 20   Sworn into his seat in the Forty First Congress. Was appointed to the Committee on Banking and Currency, and made its chairman. Served also on the Select Committee on the Census, and on the Committee on Rules. As Chairman of the Census Committee, Garfield urged that the Census be broadened into a great fact-gathering agency, providing the social, commercial, and economic information on which legislation might be based. His recommendations were not accepted at this time, but ten years later, many of Garfield's suggestions were incorporated into the planning of the Census of 1880. In a sense, he deserves to be known as the father of the modern Census.

March 18   Voted for the passage of the Public Credit Act which provided for the payment of government obligations in gold. Garfield was one of the floor managers of this bill, and the leading force behind its acceptance.

September 24 In an attempt to corner gold, Jay Gould and James Fisk, stock manipulators, induced Abel Rathbone Corbin, lobbyist brother-in-law of President Grant, to exert himself to prevent the government from selling gold. Despite Grant's refusal to agree, they spread the rumor that the President opposed such sales. With Grant's approval, Secretary of the Treasury George S. Boutwell ordered the sale of $4 million in gold, and the gold price plunged from 162 to 135, with the ruin of many speculators. The investigation of this incident was assigned to the Committee on Banking of which Garfield was chairman.

September 26-30 Went to New York, where he made a close study of the methods of the gold room. His committee took voluminous testimony, which Garfield summed up in a masterful report. He exonerated Grant from any wrongdoing, but castigated Gould and Fisk for trickery and ruthless treachery. Grant called Garfield to the White House and thanked him for his handling of the Gold Panic Investigation.

1870

May 31 Voted for the Ku Klux Klan Act which took cognizance of the order and similar secret societies, and was drafted to enforce the Fifteenth Amendment. On April 20, 1871, Garfield voted for a second Ku Klux Klan Act, drafted to enforce the Fourteenth Amendment.

November 4 Reelected to the House by an overwhelming majority.

1871

January 20 Sworn into his seat in the Forty Second Congress. Was appointed Chairman of the Committee on Appropriations.

1872

May 22 Voted in favor of the Amnesty Act which removed the disabilities from all but the most prominent ex-Confederates.

June 5 Attended the Republican National Convention in Philadelphia, where Grant was renominated for the Presidency. Henry Wilson of Massachusetts was named as his running mate.

July 9 The Democratic National Convention at Baltimore nominated Horace Greeley of New York for President, and B. Gratz Brown of Missouri for Vice-President. The Liberal Republicans convening in Cincinnati on May 1 also chose the Greeley-Brown ticket.

August 10- September 9 Spent most of the summer in Montana, where he had undertaken a pacification mission to the dissatisfied Indians of that region.

September 4 A *New York Sun* expose charged Garfield along with Vice-President Colfax, Vice-Presidential nominee Wilson, and other prominent politicians with accepting stock of the Crédit Mobilier (a construction company, organized in 1864 by the promoters of the Union Pacific Railroad to divert to themselves the profits from building that line) in return for political influence.

September 9 Denied the *Sun's* charges, and stated that he did not know what this newspaper was even talking about in a letter to his friend Burke A. Hinsdale.

September 16 In an interview published in the *Cincinnati Commercial,* Garfield again categorically denied that he had ever subscribed for a single share of Credit Mobilier Stock, and that he never received or saw a share of it.

November 5 Grant was elected President once again with 286 electoral votes to 66 for Greeley, and a popular majority of 763,000.

Despite the allegations of corruption, Garfield won a sixth term in Congress by a substantial majority.

December 2 After consulting with Garfield and other leading members of the Republican Party, Speaker of the House James G. Blaine moved the appointment of a special committee to investigate the Crédit Mobilier charges. The House accepted the motion without dissent, and a committee was appointed.

December 17 Congressman Oakes Ames of Massachusetts, the chief intermediary between the Union Pacific Railway and the Congressmen testified before the committee. He mentioned Garfield, and stated that Garfield had never received any shares because he had not paid for them.

1873

January 14 Testified before the committee. Garfield admitted that he had received an offer of stock, had held it in abeyance for sometime, and had then declined.

January 20 Sowrn into his seat in the Forty-Third Congress.

January 22 Congressman Ames came again before the investigating committee and this time charged that Garfield had received some money from his stock in Crédit Mobilier. Garfield again denied the charges which seem to be true.

February 18   After much deliberation, the investigating committee recommended action only in the cases of Oakes Ames, and James Brooks of New York. Both men were to be censured by the House. There was strong feeling in the House that Garfield too should be censured, but the motion to censure him was never brought to a vote, and the Crédit Mobilier scandal was soon forgotten. Fortunately for Garfield, it was an off year in which he did not have to contest his seat.

February 24   Congressman Butler introduced an amendment to the General Appropriation Bill, of which Garfield was in charge, increasing the salaries of Congressmen by fifty percent, ($5,000 to $7,500 a year) and raising the President's salary to $50,000 a year. Garfield opposed the amendment, taking the position that such an increase should only be adopted as part of a general revision of government salaries. Four days later, however, the amendment was adopted, and the salary increase made retroactive to the beginning of the existing Congress.

March 3   Grant signed the General Appropriation Bill which was derisively labeled the "Salary Grab Act." The Act aroused a storm of public indignation.

March 21   As soon as Garfield realized the bitterness of feelings that had been aroused, he returned his share of the retroactive increase to the Treasury, and published an open letter to his constituents explaining his position. The letter, however, did not appease Garfield's district, which passed a resolution of censure.

September 2   In the campaign for the governorship of Ohio, Garfield was snubbed and overlooked in the choice of speakers, his constituents still angry with him over the "Salary Grab," although, he, personally, had denounced this piece of Congressional legislation.

September 18   The failure of the powerful banking firm of Jay Cooke & Company precipitated a fall in security prices, ultimately leading to substantial unemployment, and a decline in national income. A full scale panic ensued.

1874

January 20   Led the fight for the repeal of the "Salary Grab Act."

Congress repealed the law except for the increases that had been granted the President and the Supreme Court Justices.

March 13   Became involved in a paving contract scandal in Washington. Garfield collected a $5,000 fee for helping the De Golyer-McClelland Company of Chicago get the contract for paving some of Washington's streets. Garfield served as the company's attorney, and although he had done nothing illegal, he was again implicated in a shady deal. Was not fully exonerated until 1877.

April 14   Opposed the Inflation Bill which would have permitted $44 million additional greenbacks to be issued by the Treasury Department. Garfield called on Grant to veto the bill, which the President did, but Garfield was forced to accept a compromise with the inflationists whereby the greenbacks were fixed at $382 million. (June 20, 1874.)

August 2   Renominated for his House seat by a vote of 100 to 34. The campaign for renomination had been a difficult one, as Garfield had to defend his actions in the DeGoyler pavement matter.

October 6   Reelected to Congress by a small (less than 3,000 votes) but secure majority against two opponents. However, the Democrats gained control of the House, and were to retain unbroken control for the next six years. The House being Democratic, Garfield was assigned to the Committee on Ways and Means.

1875

January 14   Supported the Resumption of Specie Payments Act, which provided for the resumption of specie payments (by January 1, 1879), and the reduction of greenbacks in circulation to $300 million.

January 20   Sworn into his seat in the Forty-Fourth Congress. Became the acknowledged leader of the Republican minority in the House, after Speaker Blaine accepted appointment to the Senate.

March 1   Cast his vote for the Civil Rights Act which guaranteed equal rights in public places without distinction of color, and forbade exclusion of Negroes from jury duty.

1876

January 12   When the victorious Democrats introduced a general Amnesty Bill, relieving ex-Confederates from the disabilities of the Fourteenth Amendment, Garfield rose in the House to express his opposition. It was the principal reply of his party. It was one of his greatest speeches and the Amnesty Bill was dead.

March 2   Secretary of War William W. Belknap resigned his office, not wishing to face impeachment proceedings in the House. A House investigation disclosed that Belknap had received bribes for the sale of trading posts in the Indian territory. Garfield felt that this incident was the last straw, and for the moment he gave up any hope of Republican victory in the Presidential campaign that was just about to begin.

March 15-   Made a trip through New England to sound out the voters
April 15   and found that his "waving the bloody shirt" oratory of January excited the people more than did the Belknap scandal. Garfield returned to Washington heartened by what he had observed, and determined to continue to revive the memories of the war as a political strategy.

June 16   Attended the Republican National Convention in Cincinnati where a dark horse candidate, Rutherford B. Hayes of Ohio was given the Presidential nomination. William A. Wheeler of New York was selected as his running mate.

June 27-29   The Democratic National Convention meeting in St. Louis selected Samuel J. Tilden of New York for President, and Thomas A. Hendricks of Indiana for Vice-President.

August 4   Replied to L.Q.C. Lamar of Mississippi who had delivered a a speech in the House condemning the Republican Reconstruction policies. Garfield defended the Republican Party, and "waved the bloody shirt" once more, calling the Democrats the party of rebellion and disunity. It was again a very successful piece of oratory.

November 7   Garfield took a very active part in the general campaign. He was reelected to the House for an eighth time, but the Presidential election was not settled on election day. Tilden had a popular vote margin of 250,000 and an electoral vote of 184, only one short of the necessary majority. Hayes had 165 electoral votes. There were 20 disputed votes (two sets of returns had been sent in from Florida, Louisiana, South Carolina, and Oregon.)

November 10   At President Grant's request, Garfield went to New Orleans with Senators John Sherman and Stanley Matthews of Ohio and other Republicans to watch the counting of the Louisiana vote.

November 14- It is probable that we shall never know just how Louisiana
December 2   would have voted under normal conditions. In any case, Garfield was instrumental in getting the vote in Louisiana changed in favor of Hayes. The Returning Board gave the disputed votes to the Republican candidate. Garfield made a special study of the West Feliciana Parish which had gone for Tilden. He gathered enough evidence to warrant the cancellation of the whole vote of the Parish. The methods used in the other doubtful states led to the same results and the twenty disputed votes were all given to Hayes.

1877

January 29-   However, the Constitution offered no clear guide for the
February 28   disputed election of 1876. As a result, a Special Electoral Commission was set up to decide the vote. There were five Representatives, five Senators, and five members of the Supreme Court on the Commission; there were seven Republicans and seven Democrats; the fifteenth member was Justice David Davis of Illinois, an independent. But, owing to his election by the Illinois State Legislature to the United States Senate, Davis was replaced by Justice Joseph Bradley, a Republican. In a strictly partisan decision, the election went to Hayes. The Democrats in Congress threatened to filibuster when they heard the decision. Garfield, who had at first opposed the Electoral Commission as unconstitutional, finally decided that his duty to his party required him to serve, and do what he could to insure the election of Hayes.

February 26   Took part in the Wormley Conference, at which the Democrats agreed to the election of Hayes on the promise that Hayes would remove the remaining Federal troops from the South, that he would appoint at least one Southerner to the Cabinet, and that the South would receive large subsidies for internal improvements. The Democrats also agreed to muster enough votes to elect Garfield as Speaker of the House. But in this, they failed, and they were never granted the subsidies that they desired.

March 2   Rutherford B. Hayes was delcared elected as the eighteenth President of the United States. In the entire process, no one had borne a more prominent part than Garfield. Hayes was inauguarated on March 5.

April 10-24   During this period, "Black Reconstruction" in the South came to an end. Radical Republicans lost control in the Southern States, and the last Federal Troops were withdrawn from Louisiana on April 24.

November 6   Democrats carried Ohio in the election of 1877. Garfield went to Hayes and told him that the party was discouraged and divided, and that he would have to consult Congressmen more freely in matters of appointments. But Hayes refused to listen. Garfield prevented an open break between the Republicans and the President by refusing for six months to call a Caucus where the rage of disappointed Congressmen would have made all their criticisms public.

1878

February 12   Delivered a speech in Congress on the anniversary of Abraham Lincoln's birth. His address was full of praise for the martyred President, and represented a departure from Garfield's earlier public remarks concerning Lincoln.

February 28   Voted against the passage of the Bland-Allison Act, sponsored by Congressman Richard P. Bland of Missouri and Senator William B. Allison of Iowa. The Act, which was finally passed over Hayes' veto, required the Secretary of the Treasury to make monthly purchases of not less than $2 million and not more than $4 million worth of silver at the market price, such purchases to be converted into standard dollars.

September 10   Delivered a very important anti-inflation speech in the House. He urged maintenance of the gold standard, and denounced the movement for free silver.

November 7   Reelected to the House for the ninth time. However, the

Democrats carried the Congressional elections of 1878, and in 1879 would be for the first time in many years in control of both the House and the Senate. Garfield's chance for the Speakership was gone.

1879

January 1   Resumption of Specie Payments began, as authorized by the Act of 1875, with no wholesale attempt to reclaim greenbacks now on par with the national dollar.

January 20   Garfield was sworn into his seat in the Forty-Sixth Congress. He was again assigned to the Committee on Ways and Means.

March 6   Called on President Hayes and urged him to support the Republican Party's position in support of retaining the Force Acts of 1865 and 1874, which the Democrats were attempting to repeal. These acts had authorized the President to use Federal troops in Congressional elections.

March 18   Called on Hayes once more, and received definite assurances that the repeal would be vetoed. Garfield then called a caucus which agreed to support the President's veto.

March 28   Hayes called on Garfield and read to him the proposed veto measure to make sure that his veto was in harmony with the speech Garfield intended to deliver the next day.

March 29   Set the tone of the debate on the Democrats proposed repeal of the Force Acts in a speech entitled, "The Attempted Revolution in Congress." Garfield denounced the Democrats attempt to repeal the Acts by the device of attaching "riders" to three appropriations bills for 1880.

May 29   Despite Garfield's efforts, the three bills accompanied by "riders" were passed by both houses. But, in fulfillment of his promise to Garfield two months before, Hayes vetoed the measures. Garfield had won a great victory for himself and his party when on June 19, the President signed the general appropriation bill with no "riders" attached.

1880

January 6   Was selected by the unanimous vote of his party associates in the Ohio Legislature to the United States Senate to succeed Allen G. Thurman.

January 20   Asked by one of Senator John Sherman's campaign managers (Sherman was trying for the Republican Presidential nomination), to come out for Sherman or indicate his preference.

January 26   Despite his apparent favoring of Blaine for the nomination, Garfield had made too many promises before his election to the Senate, and was pledged to support Sherman. He came out openly for Sherman on this day.

February 18   Sherman told Garfield that if he could not be nominated, he would transfer his entire support and strength to Garfield. It was on this basis that Garfield became a delegate at large from Ohio and consented to go to Chicago. On this same day, Wharton Barker of Philadelphia told Garfield that he was a organizing a group of Republicans to nominate him. Governor T.L. Pound of Wisconsin strongly urged Garfield to enter the race as well.

March 17   Delivered an elaborate speech in the House defending the Force Acts. Garfield stated that they were not only constitutional, but also moral. However, in order to placate the Democrats, he offered to vote for a change in the laws by which the deputies in control of local elections would be appointed by the courts in equal numbers from both parties.

April 24   Barker and Wayne McVeagh called on Garfield and told him that the Pennsylvania delegation to the National Convention would vote for him on the second ballot.

April 25   Told Barker that Sherman had asked him to place his name in nomination, and that he had agreed to do so. Barker said that Sherman could not be nominated, and that Garfield should honor his promise as if nothing was happening. Garfield agreed.

May 9   Wrote to Barker expressing his fears that Grant might be nominated. Garfield believed that if Grant was nominated, he would split the Republican Party and pave the way for a Democratic victory.

May 20   Senator Thomas F. Bayard of Delaware introduced a bill to change the operation of the Force Acts. The Bayard Bill was essentially the changes that Garfield had proposed in his March 17 speech. The bill passed the Senate and the House

(Garfield was absent that day.) When Garfield learned of the bill's passage, he went to President Hayes and urged him to veto the measure, although he actually approved of the legislation. He took this action to maintain party regularity on the question of the Force Acts, and to embarrass the Democrats.

May 25 Left Washington for the Republican National Convention in Chicago. Although he was not an avowed candidate, many important Republicans including Governors Pound of Wisconsin, A.D. Streight of Indiana, and L.A. Sheldon of Ohio were working quite openly for his nomination. The "dark horse" label usually placed on Garfield's nomination is not totally valid.

June 2 When the Republican National Convention met in Chicago, the field was open. There were essentially two factions in the party—one headed by the supporters of James G. Blaine; the other by the leader of the "Stalwarts," Roscoe Conkling, who nominated Ulysses S. Grant.

June 3 While Conkling was speaking, Garfield entered late, and the Senator from New York was interrupted by loud and continuous applause for his rival from Ohio. Such demonstrations for Garfield occurred more than once. A movement was definitely growing for Garfield.

June 4 Garfield placed John Sherman's name in nomination. Blaine had already been nominated by James F. Joy of Michigan, and Grant's name had been placed in nomination by Conkling.

June 6 The balloting began. The first ballot stood: Grant, 304; Blaine, 284; and Sherman 93. Throughout the day, the lines established on the first ballot remained substantially unbroken. Beginning with the second ballot, Garfield's name was kept constantly before the convention as he received a few votes on each ballot especially from Pennsylvania. After twenty-eight ballots the convention adjourned for the day not having reached a decision.

June 7-8 The balloting began once more. On the twenty-ninth ballot Sherman picked up 21 votes, and on succeeding ballots his votes rose to 120. But the Sherman boom was short-lived, and by the thirty-third ballot the deadlock was reestablished.

At this point, Sherman realized finally that he could not be nominated, and threw his support to Garfield as he had promised to do on February 18. He also urged all other Republicans to do likewise. On the thirty-fourth ballot Ohio, Indiana and Wisconsin voted for Garfield. Throughout all of this, Garfield had refused to allow the use of his name, but had been disregarded. On the Thirty-Sixth Ballot Garfield received 399 votes and the nomination. The "Stalwart" faction was appeased with the nomination of Chester A. Arthur of New York for Vice-President.

June 9 The Greenback Labor Party met at Chicago and nominated James B. Weaver of Iowa for President, and B.J. Chambers of Texas for Vice-President.

June 15 President Hayes vetoed the Bayard Bill according to Garfield's entreaties of May 20.

June 22 The Democratic National Convention met in Cincinnati and nominated Winfield S. Hancock of Pennsylvania for President, and William H. English of Indiana for Vice-President.

July 10 Issued a formal letter of acceptance of the nomination. Garfield promised to carry forward the cause of civil service reform. He also recognized that his greatest task was to unite his party, and heal the divisions that had been so aroused at Chicago so as to present a united front against the Democrats in November. Although a campaign committee was organized, Garfield proved to be his own efficient campaign manager.

July 15 Began his campaign at Mentor, Ohio which became the headquarters of one of the most shrewdly conducted political campaigns in history.

August 5 Met with the Republican National Committee in New York City to discuss campaign strategy. Blaine, Sherman, Levi P. Morton, John A. Logan and others attended. The absence of Senator Conkling was noticeable, but Garfield felt that Conkling probably wanted to avoid the appearance of some bargain that would limit the freedom of the candidate.

August 6 At the home of Whitelaw Reid, Garfield met with a number of powerful figures in business and politics including Jay

Gould of "Black Friday" fame. Neither man remembered that Garfield had once attacked Gould for his part in the gold scandal of 1869.

August 8   Delivered a long address at Chautauqua, New York on the subject of the tariff. Garfield came out for a high tariff, but one that would contain certain reforms.

August 9   Returned to Mentor. Garfield's right hand was very swollen from all the handshaking he had done on this short campaign trip. Received a congratulatory letter from Grant. Moreover, from this time on, Conkling and his friends began to work very hard for the success of the National Republican ticket.

September 2   Wrote to Amos Townsend of Cleveland inquiring about the support of John D. Rockefeller. Garfield asked Townsend to speak to Rockefeller so that the oil magnate would bring pressure to bear on his employees in his factories to support Garfield.

September 28   Met with Conkling and Grant at Warren, Ohio. The meeting was purely formal and there was no private conference between them. Yet, the very fact that these two high Republican leaders had come to Warren was generally regarded as a great success for party unity.

November 2   The campaign, which had not at all been sensational or dynamic, indicated that the Republican tactic of "waving the bloody shirt" was losing its effectiveness, but the revival of prosperity in 1880 favored the Republicans. As a result, when the votes were tabulated on election day, Garfield received 4,449,053; Hancock, 4,442,035; and Weaver, 308,-578. The vote in the electoral college was 214 to 155. Victories in New York and Indiana decided the extremely close election for Garfield, while the Republicans regained control of the House for the first time since 1874.

November 4   President Hayes, who was in Ohio at this time, came to Mentor to congratulate Garfield. Hayes was undoubtedly very happy over the result of the election.

November 27   Met with Blaine in Washington and offered him the post of Secretary of State, which Blaine joyfully accepted on

December 20. The selection of the rest of the Cabinet posed difficulties for Garfield. These difficulties arose in part from an East-West rivalry in the Republican Party, and in part from the development of a boss system in some of the most important states, notably New York. The political bosses demanded control over patronage appointments, and this would prove difficult for Garfield.

1881

January 24   Edwards Pierrepont of New York, a close friend of Conkling, came to Mentor and told Garfield that Conkling wanted Levi P. Morton appointed Secretary of the Treasury. Garfield said he would consider the appointment. Grant, Thomas C. Platt, and A.B. Cornell later also urged the appointment of Morton.

February 16   Conkling, himself, came to Mentor to discuss the appointment. No agreement was reached as Garfield refused to commit himself to a Morton selection.

February 19   Offered C.J. Folger, Chief Justice of the New York Supreme Court, the post of Attorney General as a concession to Conkling. But Folger declined the position on February 23.

March 1   Offered Morton the post of Secretary of the Navy. Morton accepted on the next day. Garfield believed that his chief difficulty (that of satisfying Conkling) was settled. In reality, it was not.

March 2   When Garfield reached Washington, only three positions in the Cabinet had been filled; Blaine for Secretary of State, Robert T. Lincoln for Secretary of War, and Wayne McVeagh of Pennsylvania for Attorney General. Although Morton was pleased with the post he had accepted, his political associates were not. As a result, Morton reluctantly declined the appointment. Only a day before the inauguration, Garfield appointed T.L. James of New York to the position of Postmaster General without consulting with Conkling. Conkling protested to Garfield the next day feeling he had been cheated, but received no satisfaction.

March 3   Went to the Wormley hotel where he delivered a speech to sixteen of his Williams College classmates. He also worked on his inaugural address until two thirty in the morning.

ADMINISTRATION

March 4　Was inaugurated the Twentieth President of the United States. Gave an address which revealed his scholarly qualities and his deep faith in the American system.

After the inaugural ceremonies, Garfield again took up the question of his Cabinet. Offered the Treasury to William Windom of Minnesota later that evening.

March 5　Windom accepted. Garfield then appointed S.J. Kirkwood of Iowa Secretary of the Interior and W.H. Hunt of Louisiana Secretary of the Navy. The Cabinet was now complete. Though not an ideal Cabinet, it was, nevertheless, a good one. Garfield had fought and won an important battle, for no one could say that his cabinet had been imposed on him by any political leader.

March 7　Gave Postmaster General James permission to begin an investigation of the "Star Route Frauds," which involved huge expenditures of money to deliver mail in certain thinly populated regions of the West. It was discovered that some of these routes served by stage coaches rendered almost negligible services. Yet, more than a million dollars a year was being appropriated by Congress to pay for these so-called deliveries.

March 23-
May 16　Garfield's appointments were regarded by the "Stalwarts" (Conservative Republicans) as a victory for the "Half-Breed" wing (Liberals) of the party. This struggle over the spoils of office came to a head when Garfield challenged Conkling's control of the New York patronage by naming a Conkling opponent, William H. Robertson, as Collector of the Port of New York, over the protests of Conkling and Thomas Platt, the junior Senator from New York. They succeeded in blocking the appointment until May, and then resigned (May 16) in protest. In July, the New York Legislature refused to reelect the pair. Conkling then retired from politics, and the "Stalwart" faction declined.

April 20　Demanded and received the resignation of T.W. Brady of Indiana who had been the man responsible for the "Star Route Fraud" contracts. Though most of the other guilty parties got off without punishment, the immediate effect of the revelations was to save millions of dollars a year in mail contracts, and to introduce a new tone into the conduct of government.

May 18 Robertson was confirmed as Collector of the Port of New York without a roll call. Garfield's triumph over Conkling was complete.

June 18 Went to Elberon, New Jersey to visit his wife who was seriously ill. Garfield met Grant who was visiting in the same place. Grant was very cold toward the President. After a few days rest, Garfield returned to Washington.

July 2 President Garfield was shot at the Washington railroad station by Charles J. Guiteau, a mentally deranged and disappointed office seeker who shouted that he was a "Stalwart," and wanted Chester A. Arthur for President. Garfield was going to New England to personally introduce his two sons to Williams College where they were going to enter in the fall. Garfield fell in a faint, soon recovered consciousness, and was taken to the White House.

September 6 Taken to Elberon because the heat of the summer in Washington was intense. Garfield was steadily growing weaker.

September 19 After seventy-nine days, Garfield died at Elberon. The bullet was never located, and the wound had become infected. Modern medical judgment has stated that Garfield would not have died from this wound. Garfield's death resulted in a strong wave of public opinion against "Stalwartism." Guiteau was tried on November 14, 1881, convicted, and executed on June 30, 1882.

September 20 Chester A. Arthur, the Vice-President, took the oath of office as the Twenty-First President of the United States. Garfield's body was taken to Cleveland, where it was buried.

DOCUMENTS

INAUGURAL ADDRESS
March 4, 1881

This was the only speech of importance delivered by Garfield in his short tenure as President. It was an excellent address and very well received by Congress.

FELLOW-CITIZENS: We stand to-day upon an eminence which over-looks a hundred years of national life—a century crowded with perils, but crowned with the triumphs of liberty and law. Before continuing the on-ward march let us pause on this height for a moment to strengthen our faith and renew our hope by a glance at the pathway along which our people have traveled.

It is now three days more than a hundred years since the adoption of the first written constitution of the United States—the Articles of Confederation and Perpetual Union. The new Republic was then beset with danger on every hand. It had not conquered a place in the family of nations. The decisive battle of the war for independence, whose centennial anniversay will soon be gratefully celebrated at Yorktown, had not yet been fought. The colonists were struggling not only against the armies of a great nation, but against the settled opinions of mankind; for the world did not then believe that the supreme authority of government could be safely intrusted to the guardianship of the people themselves.

We can not overestimate the fervent love of liberty, the intelligent courage, and the sum of common sense with which our fathers made the great experiment of self-government. When they found, after a short trial, that the confederacy of States was too weak to meet the necessities of a vigorous and expanding republic, they boldly set it aside, and in its stead established a National Union, founded directly upon the will of the people, endowed with full power of self-preservation and ample authority for the accomplishment of its great object.

Under this Constitution the boundaries of freedom have been enlarged, the foundations of order and peace have been strengthened, and the growth of our people in all the better elements of national life has indicated the wisdom of the founders and given new hope to their descendants. Under this Constitution our people long ago made themselves safe against danger from without and secured for their mariners and flag equality of rights on

35

all the seas. Under this Constitution twenty-five States have been added to the Union, with constitutions and laws, framed and enforced by their own citizens, to secure the manifold blessings of local self-government.

The jurisdiction of this Constitution now covers an area fifty times greater than that of the original thirteen States and a population twenty times greater than that of 1780.

The supreme trial of the Constitution came at last under the tremendous pressure of civil war. We ourselves are witnesses that the Union emerged from the blood and fire of that conflict purified and made stronger for all the beneficent purposes of good government.

And now, at the close of this first century of growth, with the inspirations of its history in their hearts, our people have lately reviewed the conditions of the nation, passed judgment upon the conduct and opinions of political parties, and have registered their will concerning the future administration of the Government. To interpret and to execute that will in accordance with the Constitution is the paramount duty of the Executive.

Even from this brief review it is manifest that the nation is resolutely facing to the front, resolved to employ its best energies in developing the great possibilities of the future. Sacredly preserving whatever has been gained to liberty and good government during the century, our people are determined to leave behind them all those bitter controversies concerning things which have been irrevocably settled, and the further discussion of which can only stir up strife and delay the onward march.

The supremacy of the nation and its laws should be no longer a subject of debate. That discussion, which for half a century threatened the existence of the Union, was closed at last in the high court of war by a decree from which there is no appeal—that the Constitution and the laws made in pursuance thereof are and shall continue to be the supreme law of the land, binding alike upon the States and the people. This decree does not disturb the autonomy of the States nor interfere with any of their necessary rights of local self-government, but it does fix and establish the permanent supremacy of the Union.

The will of the nation, speaking with the voice of battle and through the amended Constitution, has fulfilled the great promise of 1776 by proclaiming "liberty through the land to all the inhabitants thereof."

The elevation of the negro race from slavery to the full rights of citizenship is the most important political change we have known since the adoption of the Constitution of 1787. No thoughtful man can fail to appreciate its beneficent effect upon our institutions and people. It has freed us from the perpetual danger of war and dissolution. It has added immensely to the moral and industrial forces of our people. It has liberated the master as well as the slave from a relation which wronged and enfeebled both. It has surrendered to their own guardianship the manhood of more than 5,000,000 people, and has opened to each one of them a career of freedom and usefulness. It has given new inspiration to the power of self-help in both races by making labor more honorable to the one and more necessary to the other. The influence of this force will grow greater and bear richer fruit with the coming years.

No doubt this great change has caused serious disturbance to our Southern communities. This is to be deplored, though it was perhaps unavoidable. But those who resisted the change should remember that under our institutions there was no middle ground for the negro race between slavery and equal citizenship. There can be no permanent disfranchised peasantry in the United States. Freedom can never yield its fullness of blessings so long as the law or its administration places the smallest obstacle in the pathway of any virtuous citizen.

The emancipated race has already made remarkable progress. With unquestioning devotion to the Union, with a patience and gentleness not born of fear, they have "followed the light as God gave them to see the light." They are rapidly laying the material foundations of self-support, widening their circle of intelligence, and beginning to enjoy the blessings that gather around the homes of the industrious poor. They deserve the generous encouragement of all good men. So far as my authority can lawfully extend, they shall enjoy the full and equal protection of the Constitution and the laws.

The free enjoyment of equal suffrage is still in question, and a frank statement of the issue may aid its solution. It is alleged that in many communities negro citizens are practically denied the freedom of the ballot. In so far as the truth of this allegation is admitted, it is answered that in many places honest local government is impossible if the mass of uneducated negroes are allowed to vote. These are grave allegations. So far as the latter is true, it is the only palliation that can be offered for opposing the freedom of the ballot. Bad local government is certainly a great evil, which ought to be prevented; but to violate the freedom and sanctities of the suffrage is more than an evil. It is a crime which, if persisted in, will destroy the Government itself. Suicide is not a remedy. If in other lands it be high treason to compass the death of the king, it shall be counted no less a crime here to strangle our sovereign power and stifle its voice.

It has been said that unsettled questions have no pity for the repose of nations. It should be said with the utmost emphasis that this question of the suffrage will never give repose or safety to the States or to the nation until each, within its own jurisdiction, makes and keeps the ballot free and pure by the strong sanctions of the law.

But the danger which arises from ignorance in the voter can not be denied. It covers a field far wider than that of negro suffrage and the present condition of the race. It is a danger that lurks and hides in the sources and fountains of power in every state. We have no standard by which to measure the disaster that may be brought upon us by ignorance and vice in the citizens when joined to corruption and fraud in the suffrage.

The voters of the Union, who make and unmake constitutions, and upon whose will hang the destinies of our governments, can transmit their supreme authority to no successors save the coming generation of voters, who are the sole heirs of soverign power. If that generation comes to its inheritance blinded by ignorance and corrupted by vice, the fall of the Republic will be certain and remediless.

The census has already sounded the alarm in the appalling figures which mark how dangerously high the tide of illiteracy has risen among our voters and their children.

To the South this question is of supreme importance. But the responsibility for the existence of slavery did not rest upon the South alone. The nation itself is responsible for the extension of the suffrage, and is under special obligations to aid in removing the illiteracy which it has added to the voting population. For the North and South alike there is but one remedy. All the constitutional power of the nation and of the States and all the volunteer forces of the people should be surrendered to meet this danger by the savory influence of universal education.

It is the high privilege and sacred duty of those now living to educate their successors and fit them, by intelligence and virtue, for the inheritance which awaits them.

In this beneficent work sections and races should be forgotten and partisanship should be unknown. Let our people find a new meaning in the divine oracle which declares that "a little child shall lead them," for our own little children will soon control the destinies of the Republic.

My countrymen, we do not now differ in our judgment concerning the controversies of past generations, and fifty years hence our children will not be divided in their opinions concerning our controversies. They will surely bless their fathers and their fathers' God that the Union was preserved, that slavery was overthrown, and that both races were made equal before the law. We may hasten or we may retard, but we can not prevent, the final reconciliation. Is it not possible for us now to make a truce with time by anticipating and accepting its inevitable verdict?

Enterprises of the highest importance to our moral and material well-being unite us and offer ample employment of our best powers. Let all our people, leaving behind them the battlefields of dead issues, move forward and in their strength of liberty and the restored Union win the grander victories of peace.

The prosperity which now prevails is without parallel in our history. Fruitful seasons have done much to secure it, but they have not done all. The preservation of the public credit and the resumption of specie payments, so successfully attained by the Administration of my predecessors, have enabled our people to secure the blessings which the seasons brought.

By the experience of commercial nations in all ages it has been found that gold and silver afford the only safe foundation for a monetary system. Confusion has recently been created by variations in the relative value of the two metals, but I confidently believe that arrangements can be made between the leading commercial nations which will secure the general use of both metals. Congress should provide that the compulsory coinage of silver now required by law may not disturb our monetary system by driving either metal out of circulation. If possible, such an adjustment should be made that the purchasing power of every coined dollar will be exactly equal to its debt-paying power in all the markets of the world.

The chief duty of the National Government in connection with the currency of the country is to coin money and declare its value. Grave doubts have been entertained whether Congress is authorized by the Constitution to make any form of paper money legal tender. The present issue of United States notes has been sustained by the necessities of war; but such paper should depend for its value and currency upon its convenience in use and its prompt redemption in coin at the will of the holder, and not upon its compulsory circulation. These notes are not money, but promises to pay money. If the holders demand it, the promise should be kept.

The refunding of the national debt at a lower rate of interest should be accomplished without compelling the withdrawal of the national-bank notes, and thus disturbing the business of the country.

I venture to refer to the position I have occupied on financial questions during a long service in Congress, and to say that time and experience have strengthened the opinions I have so often expressed on these subjects.

The finances of the Government shall suffer no detriment which it may be possible for my Administration to prevent.

The interests of agriculture deserve more attention from the Government than they have yet received. The farms of the United States afford homes and employment for more than one-half our people, and furnish much the largest part of all our exports. As the Government lights our coasts for the production of mariners and the benefit of commerce, so it should give to the tillers of the soil the best lights of practical science and experience.

Our manufactures are rapidly making us industrially independent, and are opening to capital and labor new and profitable fields of employment. Their steady and healthy growth should still be matured. Our facilities for transportation should be promoted by the continued improvement of our harbors and great interior waterways and by the increase of our tonnage on the ocean.

The development of the world's commerce has led to an urgent demand for shortening the great sea voyage around Cape Horn by constructing ship canals or railways across the isthmus which unites the continents. Various plans to this end have been suggested and will need consideration, but none of them has been sufficiently matured to warrant the United States in extending pecuniary aid. The subject, however, is one which will immediately engage the attention of the Government with a view to a thorough protection to American interests. We will urge no narrow policy nor seek peculiar or exclusive privileges in any commercial route; but, in the language of my predecessor, I believe it to be the right "and duty of the United States to assert and maintain such supervision and authority over any interoceanic canal across the isthmus that connects North and South America as will protect our national interest."

The Constitution guarantees absolute religious freedom. Congress is prohibited from making any law respecting an establishment of religion or prohibiting the free exercise thereof. The Territories of the United States are subject to the direct legislative authority of Congress, and hence the General Government is responsible for any violation of the Constitution in any of them. It is therefore a reproach to the Government that in the most populous of the Territories the constitutional guaranty is not enjoyed by the people and the authority of Congress is set at naught. The Mormon Church not only offends the moral sense of manhood by sanctioning polygamy, but prevents the administration of justice through ordinary instrumentalities of law.

In my judgment it is the duty of Congress, while respecting to the uttermost the conscientious convictions and religious scruples of every citizen, to prohibit within its jurisdiction all criminal practices, especially of that class which destroy the family relations and endanger social order. Nor can any ecclesiastical organization be safely permitted to usurp in the smallest degree the functions and powers of the National Government.

The civil service can never be placed on a satisfactory basis until it is regulated by law. For the good of the service itself, for the protection of those who are intrusted with the appointing power against the waste of time and obstruction to the public business caused by the inordinate pressure for place, and for the protection of incumbents against intrigue and wrong, I shall at the proper time ask Congress to fix the tenure of the minor offices of the several Executive Departments and prescribe the grounds upon which removals shall be made during the terms for which incumbents have been appointed.

Finally, acting always within the authority and limitations of the Constitution, invading neither the rights of the States nor the reserved rights of the people, it will be the purpose of my Administration to maintain the authority of the nation in all places within its jurisdiction; to enforce obedience to all the laws of the Union in the interests of the people; to demand rigid economy in all the expenditures of the Government, and to require the honest and faithful service of all executive officers, remembering that the offices were created, not for the benefit of incumbents or their supporters, but for the service of the Government.

And now, fellow-citizens, I am about to assume the great trust which you have committed to my hands. I appeal to you for that earnest and thoughtful support which makes this Government in fact, as it is in law, a government of the people.

I shall greatly rely upon the wisdom and patriotism of Congress and of those who may share with me the responsibilities and duties of administration, and, above all, upon our efforts to promote the welfare of this great people and their Government I reverently invoke the support and blessings of Almighty God.

JAMES A. GARFIELD

CHESTER A. ARTHUR

CHRONOLOGY

EARLY LIFE

1830

October 5 Born: North Fairfield, Vermont as Chester Abell Arthur. Father: William; Mother: Malvina Stone.

1832

September Family moved to Williston, Vermont, where young Chester's father, a Baptist pastor, ran the local academy and the Baptist church.

1833

October Family moved again to neighbouring Hinesburgh, Vermont, and two years later, the Arthurs joined the stream of migration from Vermont to Western New York. They first lived near the Erie Canal at Perry, in Genessee County, and later at York, in Livingston County.

1839

November 6 William Arthur moved the family to Union Village (Greenwich), not far from Saratoga, where he settled down for a pastorate that lasted five years. Chester was enrolled at Union Village Academy and remained there for five years until his father retired from the Union Village pastorate in 1844.

1844

August 1 Family moved to Schenectady, where William Arthur became the pastor of the First Baptist Church there.

December 4 At the age of fourteen, Chester was an avid supporter of Henry Clay, and joined other lads in a typical tribute of the times to the Whig candidate by raising an "ash-pole." During the winter of 1844-45, he attended the Schenectady Lyceum to prepare for his entry into Union College.

1845

September 5 Entered Union College as a sophomore in good standing. Arthur's choice of a classical curriculum may be regarded as an indication of his own conservatism, or of his father's wishes. Twice during the long winter vacations, Arthur left

45

Schenectady to conduct schools in neighboring towns. In 1848, he taught at district school No. 14 in Schaghticoke and was paid $18 a month. These jobs helped him earn a portion of the costs of his education.

1848

July 23   Graduated from Union College. Upon graduation, he was elected to Phi Beta Kappa, and that seems to have been his one college honor.

August 16   Proposed to become a lawyer, and with family encouragement went first to Ballston Spa for a few months in a law school. Arthur continued his preparations by private study at home and while teaching school.

1851

September 18   Began teaching at a school in North Pownall, Vermont, not far from his family then residing at Hoosick Corners, New York. Arthur remained at North Pownall school until July, 1852.

1852

October 1   Became principal of an academy at Cohoes, New York, and remained in this position until February, 1853.

November 2   Became a Henry Clay Whig, and cast his first vote in an election for Winfield Scott for President. Scott was defeated by Franklin Pierce.

LAW AND POLITICS

1853

March 1   Entered the law office of Erastus D. Culver in New York City as a student. The firm, Culver & Parker, was located at 289 Broadway.

1854

May 1   Culver & Parker certified to the Supreme Court of New York that Arthur had completed his course of study in their offices and was "of good moral character."

May 4   Was admitted to the New York bar, and taken into the law firm as a full partner on the same day. The firm was now called Culver, Parker & Arthur.

August 16   Holding strong anti-slavery convictions, Arthur attended the "Anti-Nebraska" convention in Saratoga, from which momentum was gained for the fusion of New York Whigs with other elements outraged by the Democrats' Kansas policy.

1855

November 14   With his firm anti-slavery feelings, Arthur accepted a case involving Negro rights. Lizzie Jennings, a Negro woman had been forcibly ousted from a Brooklyn streetcar by the conductor, and others, with injury to her person and clothing. Her ejection was promoted by the demands of a white passenger. Arthur took the case, and won a judgment of $500 for Lizzie Jennings, but more important was the fact that the streetcar company instructed its conductors to allow Negroes to ride unmolested.

1856

January 20   The firm of Culver, Parker & Arthur was dissolved because Culver had been promoted to the bench in Brooklyn. Arthur and a young lawyer named Henry D. Gardiner then formed a partnership, moved to Kansas to set up their practice, but soon returned to New York City and established their offices at 117 Nassau Street. At the same time, Arthur took up residence in a family hotel at 904 Broadway, and was soon an active member of the New York Republican Party.

November 4   Took an active part in the Presidential campaign of 1856, avidly supporting the candidacy of John C. Fremont, the Republican nominee. Served on the executive committee of the Eighteenth Ward Young Men's Fremont Vigilance Committee. Arthur was also an inspector of elections at the polls, and cast his vote for Fremont who went down to defeat at the hands of the Democratic candidate James Buchanan.

1859

October 25   Married Ellen Lewis Herndon of Fredericksburg, Virginia, and moved into a house at Fourth Avenue and Twenty-First Street, where the Arthurs lived until the outbreak of the Civil War in 1861. During these years, Arthur joined the New York Militia, and became Judge-Advocate-General of the Second Brigade.

1860

November 6   Supported Abraham Lincoln for the Presidency, and as one of the lesser lieutenants of the Republican organization in New York City, he played a small part in the Lincoln victory. At the same time, he assisted in reelecting Edwin D. Morgan as Governor of New York State.

December 10 A son, William Lewis Herndon Arthur, was born.

1861

January 1 Was appointed to Governor Morgan's staff as engineer-in-chief, with the rank of Brigadier General. Arthur discharged his duties creditably.

April 12 The Civil War began with the Confederate shelling of Ft. Sumter, South Carolina. Arthur was now obliged to undertake the serious work of a military establishment.

April 13 Appointed assistant quartermaster general under Cuyler Van Vechten, quartermaster general of New York. Arthur was stationed in New York City, and was given full responsibility for supplying barracks, food, and equipment to thousands of troops.

April 18 Accomplished extraordinary things in less than a week as assistant quartermaster general. Van Vechten gave him unstinted praise for his efforts in his annual report.

November 9 A day after the *Trent* affair with Great Britain, Arthur was summoned to Albany by Governor Morgan for consultation concerning the defenses of New York Harbor. Arthur was not a professional engineer, and wished to resign. However, Morgan insisted that he retain his office and procure adequate assistance.

December 26 Summoned a board of engineers to cope with the problem. Their decision was to prevent vessels from entering the harbor by stretching across the channel an obstacle consisting of cribs of stone held together by chain cables. Arthur, on his own initiative, and without a state appropriation, bought up thousands of feet of timber with his own money. When the crisis soon passed, before the plan could be implemented, Arthur found himself in possession of a huge supply of lumber. However, the state legislature came to his aid by passing a bill authorizing the sale of unused war materials. He sold the lumber at a profit to the state.

1862

January 10 Submitted an elaborate report on the condition of the national forts both on the seacoast, and on the inland border of the state. Arthur also drew up plans for the protection of the entire state, and although his proposals were thorough and definite, the legislature did not adopt his ambitious program.

April 14   Received a commission from Governor Morgan as inspector-general of New York troops in the field.

April 19   General Irwin McDowell captured the town of Fredericksburg, Virginia.

May 2   Arthur inspected the New York troops in McDowell's corps at Fredericksburg, and visited his wife's family home there, seeking to relieve their misfortunes somewhat.

May 14   Inspected the New York troops in General George C. McClellan's Army of the Potomac on the Chickahominy. There his principal task was to discover the steps required to recruit the depleted New York regiments up to full strength.

June 1   As McClellan was about to advance on Richmond, Arthur was summoned back to New York by an urgent message from Governor Morgan, although he had planned to remain with McClellan and see some action.

June 30   Acted as secretary of the meeting of the governors of the loyal states which was held at the Astor House in New York City. Secretary of State William Seward, Governor Morgan, Governor John Curtin of Pennsylvania, and others were in attendance.

June 2   As a result of the meeting, Lincoln was asked by the governors to summon more troops. On this day, the President issued his famous call for "three-hundred thousand more."

July 27   Received a commission from Governor Morgan as quartermaster general. Arthur's job was to raise 120,000 men, all to be trained, and sent to the front as quickly as possible. Until he retired from this office on December 31, 1862, Arthur performed his service quite admirably, completing all the tasks set before him.

1863

January 1   Arthur made his final report as quartermaster general to the new Democratic Governor of New York State, Horatio

Seymour who praised him on the excellent job that he had done.

January 26 Returned to the practice of law with his partner Henry C. Gardiner, with whom he remained until 1867. Arthur quickly expanded the law practice and brought in large fees.

July 8 Arthur's son, William Lewis Herndon, died of convulsions at Englewood, New Jersey.

1864

June 12 Appeared before several Congressional Committees as a claims representative for persons seeking reimbursements and damages growing out of the war. In fact, the firm of Arthur & Gardiner flourished as a result of their absorbing practice as claims agents. During the last year of the war they acquired a modest fortune and a legal reputation which was of great advantage when the war terminated.

July 25 A second son, William, was born in New York City.

1865

April 9 General Robert E. Lee surrendered to General Ulysses S. Grant at Appomattox Court House.

April 14 President Lincoln was assassinated at Ford's Theater in Washington, D.C. The President's murder plunged the country into a morass of reconstruction vindictiveness, and in New York the conservative Republicans were swept out of office by the radicals in the Congressional and State elections of 1866.

1867

January 25 Elected to the Century Club, a group distinguished in intellectual and social life. Some of its members included William Evarts, Joseph Choate, E.L. Godkin, Andrew D. White, Edwin Booth, J. Pierpont Morgan, and William C. Whitney. The reconstruction period brought continued prosperity to Arthur, and he moved into the better circles of society. He also took a recognized place among the city's Republican Party leaders.

June 6 Arthur's brother William was married to Alice Bridge Jackson in Boston. Chester attended the wedding.

August 10   At the Republican State Convention, Senator Roscoe Conkling undertook to unite the Conservative and Radical factions of the New York Republican Party. He also wanted to become the only Republican "boss" of the state. While Conkling's unification was temporarily delayed, in the in the succeeding months many New York conservatives became his followers. Among them, Arthur was becoming prominent.

1868

November 3   Ulysses S. Grant was elected the eighteenth President of the United States having defeated the Democratic candidate Horatio Seymour. During the campaign, Arthur headed the Executive Committee of the New York City Republican Party organization. He was also the Chairman of the Central Grant Club, and of the Executive Committee of the Republican State Committee. He had become one of Conkling's most trusted lieutenants.

1869

February 1   Appointed to the post of counsel to the New York City Tax Commission with a salary of $10,000 year. It was an obvious political plum, but Arthur resigned the post in August, 1870 when William Marcy Tweed (a Democratic boss) gained control over the state legislature.

1871

September 25   Attended the Republican State convention at Syracuse, New York where he supported the Conkling wing of the party which thereafter dominated the entire state organization.

November 20   President Grant appointed Arthur to the post of Collector of the Port of New York which he reluctantly accepted. On the same day, his only daughter, Ellen, was born.

1872

January 1   Formed the law firm of Arthur, Phelps & Knevals.

May 1   Convening at Cincinnati, the Liberal Republicans nominated Horace Greeley of New York for President and B. Gratz Brown of Missouri for Vice-President. On July 9, the Democratic National Convention at Baltimore also picked the Greeley-Brown slate.

June 5 Attended the Republican National Convention at Philadelphia where Grant was renominated. Henry Wilson of Massachusetts was given second place on the ticket.

November 5 Grant and Wilson were elected by a popular majority of 763,000 votes over Greeley and Brown. The Conkling-Arthur Republican machine had been instrumental in winning New York State for Grant.

1874

November 7 Despite Arthur's New York machine, a Democrat, Samuel J. Tilden was elected Governor by 50,000 votes. A reaction against Republicanism had followed very shortly after the reelection of Grant in 1872.

1875

November 4 New York State went Democratic again as the revelations of corruption in the Grant Administration hurt the Republican's chances of winning back the state. Arthur was forced to leave the campaign in October to go to his father at Newtonville during his last illness. Death came on October 27.

December 17 Was reappointed Collector of the Port of New York by Grant, and was confirmed by the Senate on the same day without reference to a committee, a courtesy never before extended to an appointee who had not been a Senator.

1876

March 22 At the New York State Republican Convention at Syracuse, Arthur led the fight for an endorsement of Roscoe Conkling's candidacy for President. Althought there was considerable opposition to this plan, Arthur's machine won the endorsement by a vote of 250 to 113.

June 8 Arrived in Cincinnati to represent Conkling's interests at the Republican National Convention. He had made the trip with DeWitt C. Wheeler and Stephen B. French, all three belonging to the Conkling "camp." None were official delegates, but they lobbyed for Conkling's nomination during the next eight days.

June 16 When it became obvious that Conkling could not win the nomination, Arthur and his associates persuaded the New York delegation to transfer its votes to Rutherford B. Hayes who was nominated for the Presidency on the seventh ballot. William A. Wheeler of New York was given second place on the ticket much to the dismay of the Arthur forces since Wheeler was not a member of the machine.

June 28-29   The Democratic National Convention meeting in St. Louis nominated Samuel J. Tilden of New York and Thomas A. Hendricks of Indiana for President and Vice-President respectively.

August 23   Attended the New York State Republican Convention at Saratoga to choose a state ticket. The management of the convention fell upon Arthur who had gone as the active controller of a majority of New York City delegates. Arthur handled the job poorly, and ex-Governor Edwin Morgan finally received the nomination for Governor, although the leading aspirant for the machine had been Alonzo B. Cornell.

November 7-   Despite the setbacks at Cincinnati and Saratoga, Arthur
December 6   worked zealously in behalf of the party's nominees. But the Republicans lost New York anyway. Tilden ran nearly 30,000 votes ahead of Hayes, and Morgan was defeated by Lucius Robinson. Hayes finally became President as a result of the Electoral Commission's decision of January 29, 1877.

1877

March 4   President Hayes proclaimed in his inaugural address that a reform in the civil service should be thorough, radical and complete. A break between the machine Republicans of New York and the President was beginning to manifest itself.

April 9   An investigation of the principal Customs Houses was begun by the Hayes Administration. Arthur began to come under attack by various reform groups. He was charged with being inefficient, neglectful, and a political hack.

April 13   Arthur was naturally indignant, and defended his control over the collectorship by denying all charges made against him and his subordinates.

April 25   A special investigating commission headed by John Jay of New York was appointed to scrutinize all Customs Houses and their officials. Arthur was allowed to help select the members of the special commission in a friendly gesture by the Hayes Administration.

May 1-2   Arthur appeared before the commission and defended his administration of the New York Customs House.

May 15   The Commission completely exonerated Arthur of any wrong-doing in a published report. However, the Commission, in later reports, stated that Arthur had lacked good judgment on several occasions as Collector, and had not vigorously supervised his Customs House.

September 26 Attended the Republican State Convention at Rochester and helped to defeat a resolution endorsing the Hayes Administration. In doing this, Arthur was not only showing his dislike for Hayes, but also publicly flouting an executive order of June 22, 1877 forbidding government officials to participate in political management.

October 24   Hayes Nominated Theodore Roosevelt for Collector to replace Arthur. The President also nominated Edwin A. Merritt for Surveyor to replace George H. Sharpe, and L. Bradford Prince for Naval Officer to replace Alonzo B. Cornell. But the three nominees were not confirmed at the Special Session of Congress.

December 11   Merritt's nomination was confirmed, but Roosevelt's and Prince's were again rejected. Arthur continued in office, trying to meet the criticisms of the Jay Commission, and to purify his staff.

1878

July 11   Arthur and Cornell were suspended from their offices by Hayes who temporarily appointed Surveyor Merritt and Silas W. Burt to become collector and Naval officer respectively.

July 19   Arthur officially relinquished his office to his successor after six years of active life and power. The Merritt and Burt appointments were not successfully approved by the Senate until

February 3, 1879 as Conkling was able to effectively block their confirmation until this date.

September 26 Attended the Republican State Convention at Saratoga. Arthur's mastery of New York City politics did not cease when he retired from the Customs House. He dictated the nomination of Edward Cooper for mayor, and successfully engineered Cooper's election in November.

1879

January 21 With Arthur's help, Conkling was elected Senator by the State Legislature for a third time. Arthur now completely dominated the New York City Republican organization and was second only to Conkling on the state level.

September 20 The Republican State Convention met at Saratoga. Arthur supported Cornell's nomination for Governor, and the Convention concurred. It went on to nominate a whole slate of machine candidates, and Arthur became Chairman of the State Committee.

November 9 Cornell was elected Governor over John Kelly, and Lucius Robinson. Arthur had done an excellent job, and began to be thought of for the Senatorship falling vacant at the expiration of Senator Francis J. Kernan's term in March, 1881.

1880

January 12 Arthur's wife, Ellen Herndon Arthur, died of pneumonia in New York City. Arthur was inconsolable as life now seemed purposeless.

February 25 Arthur, acting for the State Committee, summoned the Republican Convention for electing and instructing delegates-at-large to meet at Utica. Arthur was chosen a delegate, and he, Conkling and their associates advocated the nomination of Grant for the Presidency once again. The Arthur-Conkling forces pushed through a resolution favoring Grant, but the "Half Breed" (liberal) faction of the New York State Republican Party threatened to rebel against the bulldozing tactics of the "Stalwart" wing.

June 2-9   The Republican National Convention met at Chicago. Arthur attended as a delegate-at-large. He supported Grant to the end, but on the thirty-sixth ballot James A. Garfield of Ohio was given the nomination.

June 8   In designating a candidate for Vice-President, Garfield's friends sought to make "Stalwart" aid sure by choosing one of that faction. After Levi P. Morton declined the nomination, the New York delegation decided to propose Arthur for Vice-President. Conkling opposed this decision, but Arthur desired the nomination and defied the Senator. General Stewart L. Woodford placed Arthur's name ir nomination, and Governor William Dennison of Ohio delivered the seconding speech. Arthur was nominated by the convention on the first ballot defeating Elihu Washburne of Illinois, Marshall Jewell of Connecticut, and several others.

June 11   Arrived in New York from Chicago. Fifteen hundred welcoming admirers greeted him at Grand Central Depot.

June 22   The National Democratic Convention meeting at Cincinnati nominated Winfield S. Hancock of Pennsylvania and William H. English of Indiana for President and Vice President respectively.

July 11   Garfield and Arthur exchanged letters discussing the importance of gaining the support of the "Stalwart" faction of the Republican Party. As of this date, Arthur, as a mediator between Garfield and the "Stalwarts," seemed ineffective.

August 5   Garfield, Arthur, and a number of other top Republican leaders met at the Fifth Avenue Hotel in New York City to discuss campaign strategy for New York State. Conkling was conspicuously absent.

September 17 Conkling finally began to actively campaign for the Republican ticket, although he consistently praised Arthur more than Garfield. However, the breach in Republican ranks was rapidly being closed.

November 2   Arthur strenuously campaigned in New York. His efforts paid off as New York and the nation gave Republican majorities. Garfield and Arthur defeated Hancock and

English. Following the election, Arthur's course of action was not materially altered by his new station.

1881

January 10   The elevation of Arthur to the Vice Presidency opened the way for other "Stalwarts" to seek the Senatorship to which he had earlier aspired. However, for once in its history, the New York Republican machine could not agree on a candidate. Arthur favored Richard Crowley, while Governor Cornell supported Thomas C. Platt. The conflict between Arthur and Cornell was clearly emphasized when Arthur went to Albany on Crowley's behalf. Although the Vice-President Elect, Arthur still thought of himself as the New York Republican leader bound to fulfill political obligations and maintain organization supremacy.

January 16   Arthur lost this political fight as Platt was elected to the Senate by the State Legislature. Although Platt was a Conkling man, he was pledged to sustain nominations made in response to "Halfbreed" desires.

February 11   Was the guest speaker at a testimonial dinner for Senator Stephen W. Dorsey at Delmonico's in New York. Arthur unquestionably damaged his national reputation as a result of this speech. It was lacking in taste, and exhibited a callous disregard for public sentiment by praising Dorsey, a former "Carpetbagger."

February 24   Went to Washington, where he was escorted through the Senate chamber by outgoing Vice President William A. Wheeler. He was greeted by a number of Senators including Conkling, Hannibal Hamlin of Maine, and George H. Pendleton of Ohio among others.

VICE PRESIDENT

March 4   Was sworn into the office of the Vice President. Arthur then went to the Senate, called the new Senate to order, and swore in the new Senators before adjournment to the outdoor platform for President Garfield's oath and inaugural address.

March 5   The Senate convened with Arthur in the chair. It had been summoned to confirm Garfield's nominations to the Cabinet and lesser offices, and to consider treaties awaiting ratification.

March 23-
May 16

The "Stalwart"—"Halfbreed" struggle came to a head as a result of Garfield's cabinet appointments and the President's attempt to challenge Conkling's control over the New York patronage system. Arthur, as Vice President, cast several deciding votes which blocked the confirmation of a number of Garfield appointments. He consistently upheld the "Stalwart" cause, and supported Conkling in his struggle with the President over the patronage in New York. He, Conkling and Platt succeeded in blocking the confirmation of William H. Robertson as Collector of the Port of New York. However, Robertson was finally confirmed in May, and Conkling and Platt resigned from the Senate in protest on May 16, assuming that the New York Legislature would quickly reelect them.

May 22

Arthur went to New York to consult with other "Stalwart" leaders upon their course of action. The meeting took place at Arthur's Lexington Avenue house. It was agreed that they would go to Albany to seek the vindication of Conkling and Platt.

May 27

Arthur went to Albany to campaign for Conkling. He was bitterly attacked by the press for his actions. The newspapers called him a "bootblack for Conkling and Platt," and stated that he was demeaning the office of the Vice President.

July 1

By this date, Conkling and Platt had been defeated for reelection to the Senate from New York. Conkling retired from politics, and this event spelled the decline of the "Stalwart" faction.

July 2

Arthur remained in office, his national reputation further lowered by his continued adherence to the New York "Stalwart" group, and especially by his recent activities in Albany. His popularity declined still further, when on this day, Garfield was shot down by a crazed and disappointed office seeker, Charles J. Guiteau who shouted, "I am a Stalwart of Stalwarts . . . Arthur is President now."

September 19

President Garfield died in Elberon, New Jersey. Arthur was rather reluctant in assuming the office of the President.

ADMINISTRATION

September 20 Took the oath of office at his residence in New York before Judge John R. Brady of the New York Supreme Court.

September 21 Went with Garfield's Cabinet to Elberon to pay tribute to the dead President. Left for Washington in the afternoon.

September 22 Arthur again took the oath of office in the Vice President's room in the Capitol. This time it was administered by Chief Justice M.R. Waite. Arthur then read a brief inaugural address. A cabinet meeting was then held, and Arthur signed a proclamation declaring a day of national mourning for President Garfield's burial. Members of the cabinet were requested to retain their positions until Congress should meet in December, and it was agreed that a Special Session of the Senate should be called for October 10, 1881.

September 28-30 Held conferences in Washington and New York with his law partners, and arranged to be released from all demands upon his time. Since the White House was not ready for occupancy, Arthur set up temporary working and living quarters at the home of Senator John P. Jones of Nevada.

October 8-9 Conkling came to Washington for a meeting with the new President whose most serious concern was the choice of advisors and agents. The political gossips wrote columns of speculation.

October 10 The Senate assembled in Special Session called by Arthur. Senator Pendleton moved to elect Thomas F. Bayard of Delaware the President Pro Tem, but the Republicans blocked his election. On the next day, however, after three new Republican Senators had been sworn into office, the Republicans, now in a majority, promptly installed the Independent Senator from Illinois, David Davis, as President Pro Tem. Arthur was then notified that the Senate was organized, and the work of the session was taken up as rapidly as possible.

October 12 Sent a Special Message to the Senate concerned with the proceedings of the International Sanitary Conference which had just concluded its meetings in Washington.

October 19 Went to Yorktown, Virginia, for the centennial celebration of the British surrender. Delivered his first public speech since his inaugural. It was a brief address with no political significance.

October 24   Issued a letter of instruction to United States ministers in Europe relative to protecting the rights and interests of the United States in the projected interoceanic canal in Panama.

October 25   With Arthur's accession to the Presidency, the "Halfbreeds" and Independents began leaving the Cabinet. Arthur's choices, however, showed surprising caution and independence of the "Stalwarts." Appointed Edwin D. Morgan of New York to replace William Windom of Minnesota as Secretary of the Treasury. When Morgan declined the post because of ill health, Arthur named Charles J. Folger of New York who was immediately confirmed by the Senate.

October 26   Transmitted to the Sentate for ratification a convention between the United States and Rumania defining the rights, immunities, and privileges of consular officers.

November 4   Issued a proclamation declaring November 24 as a national day of Thanksgiving and prayer.

November 8   Wayne MacVeagh, the Attorney General, resigned. Benjamin H. Brewster of Pennsylvania was named by Arthur and confirmed on December 19, 1881.

December 6   Delivered his first Annual Message to Congress. It was a long report dealing primarily with foreign affairs.

December 12   Secreretary of State James G. Blaine resigned and was replaced by Frederick T. Frelinghuysen of New Jersey.

December 15   Submitted to the Senate a report from the Secretary of State concerning a proposed modification of the Clayton-Bulwer Treaty of 1850. Also submitted to the Senate for ratification a treaty of peace, friendship and commerce between the United States and the Kingdom of Madagascar.

December 24   Appointed Timothy O. Howe of Wisconsin to replace T.L. James of New York as Postmaster-General.

December 25   Appointed Henry M. Teller of Colorado to replace Samuel J. Kirkwood of Iowa as Secretary of the Interior, and

William E. Chandler of New Hampshire to replace W. H. Hunt as Secretary of the Navy.

1882

January 11   Transmitted to the Senate for ratification a treaty between the United States and the Shoshone and Bannock Indians regarding the disposal of some of their lands in the Ft. Hall Indian Reservation in Idaho, for use by the Utah and Northern Railroad.

January 18   Approved the sale of the Otoe and Missouria Indian Reservation to private interests in the states of Nebraska and Kansas. He also urged Congress to create the office of Medical Inspector for the United States Indian Service in order to improve the conditions of Indians occupying reservation lands.

January 19   Recommended to Congress an appropriation of $350,000 for the purchase of a site and the erection of a fireproof building to contain the records, museum, and library of the Surgeon-General's office.

January 24   Sent to the Senate for ratification a treaty of amity and commerce between the United States and the Kingdom of Serbia.

January 25   Charles J. Guiteau was found guilty of murder, and several days later was sentenced to death. He was hanged on June 30, 1882.

January 26   Urged Congress to increase its efforts in bringing about peace between Chile, Peru, and Bolivia who were then feuding among themselves over conflicting claims to certain mineral lands on their common borders.

February 2   Sent Special Message to Congress concerning the great amount of lawlessness prevailing in the Territory of Arizona, and urged Congress to enact legislation which would enable the federal government to assist the local authorities of the territory in restoring and maintaining order.

February 15   Approved a bill appropriating $50,000 for the purpose of improving educational facilities in Alaska.

February 18   Appointed Roscoe Conkling to fill a vacancy on the Supreme Court. The nomination was confirmed by the Senate, but

Conkling declined the appointment, and Arthur appointed Samuel Blatchford of New York to the post on March 1, 1882.

February 28   Sent a communication to Congress requesting additional monies for the Civil Service Commission so as to promote greater efficiency in the different branches of the civil service.

March 3   Urged Congress to approve United States participation in the Geneva Convention of 1864 and 1868.

March 7   Recommended to Congress an increase of 500 enlisted men for the naval service.

March 10   Signed a bill making certain debts incurred by American soldiers a lien against their pay.

March 13   Sent Special Message to Congress urging additional legislation to prevent the introduction of contagious and infectious diseases into the United States from foreign countries.

March 18   Sent federal troops into Nebraska at the request of the Governor of that state. Domestic violence had broken out among homesteaders and cattlemen.

March 29   Urged Congress to enact legislation to prevent trespassing on Indian lands in the west. Also approved plans for the construction of a new military post at Ft. Lewis, Colorado.

March 30   Established diplomatic relations with the government of Persia.

April 4   Vetoed a bill to restrict the admission of Chinese in accordance with a revised treaty with China. The bill prohibited the immigration of Chinese for twenty years, although the treaty between the two countries acknowledged the right of the United States to regulate, limit or suspend for what had been understood to be a briefer period.

April 7   Went to New York to see friends and relatives, and while there, ordered the adoption of a "President's flag." Returned to Washington on April 11.

April 11   Approved a bill for the continuing improvement of the water-power pool at the Rock Island Arsenal in Illinois.

April 12	Confirmed the decision of the Department of the Interior in setting aside lands in the Indian Territory for the Cheyenne and Arapahoe nations.
April 17	Sent Special Message to Congress requesting an appropriation of $1,010,000 for the Mississippi River Commission to be used for closing existing gaps in levees, improvement of navigation, and for the protection of the people of the valley from floods.
April 18	Extended an invitation to all the independent countries of North and South America to participate in a general congress to be held in Washington on November 22 for the purpose of considering and discussing the methods of preventing war between the nations of America.
	Proposed a convention between the United States and Mexico for defining the boundary between the two countries from the Rio Grande River to the Pacific Ocean.
April 25	Recommended to Congress the sending of a delegation and exhibition to the International Fisheries Exhibition to be held in London in May, 1883.
April 26	Sent Special Message to Congress concerned with the alarming and continued state of disorder and lawlessness in the Territory of Arizona. He blamed the difficulties there on armed bands of desperadoes known as "Cowboys" who not only raided Arizona towns, but also crossed the border into Mexico to spread havoc.
May 2	Asked Congress for a resolution condemning the persecution of Jews in Russia.
May 5	Approved plans to dispose of the Ft. Dodge Military Reservation in Kansas.
May 6	Signed a second Chinese Exclusion Act which set ten years as the period of suspension, and included the denial of state and national citizenship to all Chinese.
June 16	Signed an Extradition Treaty with the government of Belgium providing for the reciprocal surrender of fugitives from justice.

June 19   Signed a bill enlarging the Pawnee Indian Reservation in the Indian Territory.

June 23   Sent to Congress for ratification a treaty between the United States and Spain providing for reciprocal protection for trade marks and manufactured articles of their respective citizens and subjects.

July 1   Vetoed another act regulating the carriage of immigrants to the United States by sea. The bill was designed to apply to steamships the requirements hitherto exacted of sailing vessels in the same service. Arthur felt the bill was ill-adapted to the purpose for which it had been drawn.

July 20   Submitted to Congress for ratification a convention with Mexico providing for the reopening and retrying of the claims of Benjamin Weil and LaAbra Silver Mining Company against Mexico.

July 29   Transmitted to the Senate for ratification a commercial treaty between the United States and the Kingdom of Korea.

August 1   Vetoed a Rivers and Harbors Bill carrying a total appropriation of $18,743,875 because he felt that it contained appropriations for purposes not for the common defense or general welfare, and which did not promote commerce among the states. The bill was a typical piece of pork barrel legislation, and Arthur's veto was applauded by the public and the press.

August 3   Approved an act ordering the first generally selective restriction, with the expense of receiving and caring for the newcomers to be defrayed by a "head money" tax of fifty cents per immigrant.

August 13   Ordered the reorganization of the Military Academy at West Point, whereby the Corps of Cadets henceforth would be the responsibility of the General of the Army under the War Department.

August 15   Left for a vacation which was spent in almost perpetual motion. He visited his brother at Governor's Island, New York, commenced a round of travels, held cabinet meetings at his Lexington Avenue house or in Washington, and traveled into New England and to Alexandria Bay.

October 5   Celebrated his fifty-second birthday at Alexandria Bay where he had gone with Robert G. Dun, a friend, to fish for bass.

October 10   Met with his cabinet at his home in New York City, and in the afternoon began a brief trip to Massachusetts with Secretary of the Navy Chandler and Secretary of War Robert T. Lincoln for the centennial celebration of Daniel Webster's birthday.

November 5   In the Congressional elections, the Republicans throughout the country were beaten very badly. Congress was Democratic controlled, and in some traditionally Republican states, the Democratic Party made appreciable gains. The nation had rebuked the Arthur Administration. As if to add insult to injury, Arthur's home state of New York emphatically elected a Democratic Governor, Grover Cleveland of Buffalo. To Arthur, the outcome in New York was a political reverse of the first order, while the prestige of Arthur's position was sadly diminished by the election which now deprived his party of its control of Congress.

December 4   The nine man Tariff Commission which Arthur had appointed on May 15 recommended substantial tariff reductions.

Delivered his Second Annual Message to Congress. Again, a large part of it was devoted to foreign affairs, but other matters such as the coinage of silver, excise taxes, the condition of the navy, and Indian affairs were discussed.

December 7   The second trial of those involved in the Star Route Frauds began. The first trial which had begun during Garfield's Administration, and had dragged on into the first year of Arthur's Administration had ended inconclusively in September, 1882. The new trial continued for several months not ending until June 14, 1883 when all of the defendants were acquitted for lack of evidence. Yet, the Star Route disclosures and trials had allowed Arthur to drive the accused men from government service, while the Post Office Department was improved in its personnel, and the government was saved some $500,000 annually.

December 27 Announced to Congress that construction of a capitol building in Santa Fe, New Mexico had begun.

1883

January 10 Approved an Extradition Treaty between the United States and the government of Spain.

The Senate began its debate on the Tariff Reduction Bill. After several months, no real tariff reforms had been secured.

Gave an elegant dinner at the White House for ex-President Grant and his wife. Arthur's dinners in Washington were gala affairs, and it may be said that he began the custom of elaborate White House entertaining.

January 13 The President's youngest sister, Mrs. John McElroy arrived in Washington with her daughters. She was to become Arthur's official hostess at the executive mansion.

January 16 The last thing the public expected from President Arthur was leadership or sincere support of the civil service reform cause. His record as a machine politician seemed to augure ill for any kind of reform. Yet, it was Arthur who helped lead the fight for civil service reform as President, and on this date he signed the Pendleton Act, the first great step toward a merit system. The act was drafted by Dorman B. Eaton, Secretary of the Civil Service Reform Association, and sponsored by Senator George H. Pendleton of Ohio. It provided for a bi-partisan 3-man Civil Service Commission for drawing up and administering competitive examinations to determine on a merit basis the fitness of appointees to Federal office. A limited classified civil service list was set up, which the President was empowered to extend at his discretion. The act forbade the levying of political campaign assessments on Federal office holders and protected the latter against dismissal for failure to make such contributions. Despite various weaknesses, the Pendleton Act enabled Arthur and succeeding Presidents to broaden the merit system, and provided the foundation for the Federal Civil Service in its present form.

January 25 The House began debate on the Tariff Reduction Bill, and although President Arthur pleaded for tariff reform, his pleas fell on deaf ears.

January 26   Signed a bill which permitted bankers to sue in the Court of Claims for the amount of internal revenue tax collected from them without lawful authority.

January 27   The Marquis of Lorne, Governor General of Canada, was entertained at the White House in a lavish banquet and gay round of parties.

February 3   Transmitted to the Senate for consideration and ratification a treaty of commerce between the United States and Mexico.

February 5   Signed a bill which imposed fairly severe penalties, including imprisonment, for unlawful entry upon any Indian lands in the United States.

February 6   Attended the wedding of Alice Blaine, the daughter of James G. Blaine, in Washington. Then, in the early evening attended the wedding of Attorney General Brewster's daughter, Mary. A serious accident almost occurred when the President's carriage, on the way to the wedding, was rammed by another carriage from the rear. But, the President escaped unharmed, and walked back to the White House, after the ceremony was over, to host the Army-Navy reception.

February 9   Requested the Senate to ratify a Franco-American Claims Convention.

February 15   Went to New York City to attend the funeral of his old political friend, Ex-Governor, Edwin D. Morgan.

February 20   Asked Congress to appropriate $15,000 to be used for the construction of a sea wall on Governors Island in New York Harbor.

February 21   Appointed Leroy D. Thoman of Ohio, John M. Gregory of New York, and Dorman B. Eaton as the three members of the new Civil Service Commission. Arthur named Eaton, Chairman of the Commission on the next day.

February 22   Attended a concert in the White House given by Adelina Patti on the occasion of George Washington's birthday.

March 1 In accordance with the provisions of the Pendelton Act, Arthur named Silas W. Burt of New York to be the Chief Examiner of the Civil Service Commission. Burt, however, declined the post. Appointed Elihu Root of New York City to be the new United States Attorney General in New York replacing Stewart L. Woodford who had nominated Arthur for Vice President. As a result of this action, Arthur was called an ingrate by the "Stalwarts."

March 3 Signed the so-called "Mongrel Tariff" of 1883, which lowered duties by five percent, but retained protectionist principles. He signed it with serious misgivings having desired further reductions.

Arthur began his struggle with Congress for the improvement and modernization of the navy. On this date he approved the construction of three new steel cruisers, and one dispatch boat. On August 5, 1882, he had asked Congress for a much larger appropriation to be used for the construction of six new vessels. This request was denied.

March 9 Despite the Burt incident, the Civil Service Commission held its first meeting in Washington, and began its work with assurances of Arthur's support.

March 25 Postmaster General Howe died, and was replaced by Walter Q. Gresham of Indiana, although the "Stalwarts" of New York wanted Arthur to appoint Richard Crowley to the post. Arthur's independence was losing "Stalwart" support.

April 12 Appointed a Gun-Foundry Board to investigate the new innovations in naval ordnance as part of his plans for an improved navy. The Board visited England, France and Russia, but were denied admission to the Krupp factories in Essen, Germany. The Board also began an examination of the navyyards and arsenals owned by the government to see which were suitable for adaptation to government foundries.

April 5 Left Washington and started South for a fishing vacation in Florida. The demands of his office coupled with the numerous parties and dinners were taking their toll. Arthur was tired, weak, and out of sorts.

April 16-17   Reached Jacksonville by train. Then the President transferred to a boat for a ride up the St. Johns River to Sanford. Stopped at Orlando and Kissimmee City. Arrived at Lake Tohopekaliga on April 9 to do some fishing. Left Florida on April 17.

April 19   Arrived at Savannah, Georgia where he was taken ill with chills and fever. Was confined to bed for two days. Arthur started back to Washington on April 21, still ill and very weak.

April 22   Returned to Washington, his health somewhat improved. The President did not know that he would never fully recover from this illness. To allay public fears concerning his health, Arthur held a full Cabinet meeting on April 24, and then plunged into his work once more.

May 7   By means of an Executive Order, Arthur promulgated the first rules and regulations of the Civil Service Commission. The President received great praise from the press and public alike, and hoped that his actions concerning civil service reform would lay the basis for the Presidential nomination in 1884.

May 15   In Arthur's name, the Gun-Foundry Board issued a circular letter to all steel companies in the United States inquiring as to their facilities for the production of armor plate needed for the proposed new naval vessels.

May 21   Issued an Executive Order closing all government offices for the celebration of "Decoration Day" on May 30.

May 25   Came to New York City to participate in the dedication ceremonies at the opening of the Brooklyn Bridge. His old friends in the city noted his changed physical appearance. On his return to Washington, the President went on a diet, kept earlier hours, and lightened his work load. However, no real improvement in his weakened condition was noticeable.

July 16   On this day, the Pendleton Act officially went into operation. Up to this time, Arthur utilized government offices in New York to care for his friends.

July 21-29   Left Washington on the Presidential yacht, the U.S.S. *Despatch*, for a trip to New York City to visit his relatives and friends.

July 29   Departed New York by train, and traveled by way of Washington to Louisville, Kentucky to take part in the formal opening of the Southern Exposition being held there. Left Louisville the next day to begin his vacation. His first stop was Chicago, where he joined a number of official traveling companions.

August 3   Left Chicago for newly opened Yellowstone National Park in Wyoming where he planned to stay for a month. Accompanying the President were Secretary of War Robert T. Lincoln, General Philip Sheridan, Daniel T. Rollins, a personal friend, General Anson Stager, J. Schuyler Crosby, a New Yorker serving as Territorial Governor of Wyoming, Surgeon W.H. Forwood, guides, reporters, and several army officers.

August 9-30   Toured Yellowstone Park on horseback. The President and his party covered 300 miles, camping, fishing, and hunting.

September 4   Returned to Chicago. Arthur's health and general appearaance seemed vastly improved, and his zest for public life seemed temporarily restored. He left Chicago on September 5, arriving in Washington two days later.

September 10   Issued a Proclamation announcing the proposed opening of the World's Industrial and Cotton Centennial Exposition to be held in the city of New Orleans in December, 1884 through May, 1885.

September 20   Joined his sister, Mrs. McElroy and his nieces aboard the yacht *Despatch* which was then cruising off the coast of Rhode Island. Newport society captured him at once.

September 25   Went to Bristol, Rhode Island, where he took part in the cornerstone-laying ceremony of the Burnside Memorial Hall. After a brief address, Arthur went fishing off the coast of West Island, where he caught an eighty pound bass.

October 13   Arthur announced the retirement of William T. Sherman as General-in-Chief of the Army, and the appointment of General Philip Sheridan to the vacancy. Other General staff changes were also reported.

October 26   Issued a Proclamation designating Thursday, November 29, as a day of national thanksgiving.

November 7   Announced two dozen changes in the rules and regulations of the Pendleton Act designed to strengthen, and improve the executive civil service.

November 26   Went to New York to take part in the Centennial Celebration of the withdrawal of British troops at the close of the American Revolution. Rode in the parade down Fifth Avenue, and attended a great banquet at Delmonicos that evening. He returned to Washington the next day.

December 4   Delivered his Third Annual Message to Congress. It dealt mainly with national defense (naval building), conservation, and presidential succession.

December 10   Sent seven Special Messages to Congress dealing with various aspects of the Indian problem, including improvement of reservations, Indian timber lands, and the right of way for several railroads through Indian territory.

December 17   Sent nine Special Messages to Congress dealing with Indian relief, Indian health, and Indian appropriations.

December 19   Signed a treaty of commerce between the United States and Great Britain, and a treaty of extradition between the United States and the Grand Duchy of Luxemburg.

1884

January 4-5   As the year 1884 dawned, the subject of major public interest became the presidential campaign. Arthur wanted the nomination of his party, and journeyed to New York to consult with Republican leaders concerning his candidacy. While he was not able to gain a firm commitment from the New York Republicans, he did receive some assurances of support. Other Republicans who had declared their intentions for the nomination were John Sherman of Ohio, John A. Logan of Illinois, George F. Edmunds of Vermont, and James G. Blaine.

January 8   Reported to Congress that the State of Illinois had ceded the Illinois and Michigan Canal to the Federal government on the condition that it would be enlarged and maintained as a national waterway for commercial purposes.

January 14   Signed a bill transferring the Seminole Indians of Florida to the Creek Indian reservation in the Oklahoma Territory.

January 15   As part of his departure from traditional American foreign policy, President Arthur continued his innovation of signing treaties of commercial reciprocity with foreign nations. On this day, he signed a reciprocity treaty with Cuba and Puerto Rico.

January 17   Approved the plans for a relief expedition to aid Lieutenant A.W. Greeley and his party who had been exploring the Lady Franklin Bay region in the Arctic, and and who were now experiencing considerable difficulties.

January 28   Signed a bill appropriating $42,000 to explore the possibilities of removing Flood Rock, in the East River, New York.

February 7   Submitted to Congress the first annual *Report* of the Civil Service Commission which by this date already controlled the appointment of 13,924 Federal offices. Arthur's accompanying letter gave great praise to the work of the Commission.

February 8   Announced that General Sherman, having reached the age of 64, had been placed on the retired list of the Army without reduction in his pay or allowances.

February 13   Transmitted to Congress a memorandum concerning the settlement of the boundary line between the United States and the State of Texas.

February 14   Issued a Proclamation stating that the Spanish government had removed all discriminating customs duties imposed upon American goods, and that the United States would remove all discriminating duties on products of Spanish origin.

February 21   Announced that the British government had joined in the relief expedition being sent to aid Lieutenant Greeley and had presented the United States with the Arctic steamship *Alert* to carry on the search.

March 3   The Forty-Eighth Congress convened with the Republicans controlling the Senate, and the Democrats in control of the House. President Arthur had very little control over the decisions of this Congress, who constantly cut his appropriations requests, and as a result accomplished very little during its two years in power.

March 6   Susan B. Anthony and about a hundred delegates from a woman suffrage convention called on Arthur at the White House. She told him that if he wanted to be President for four more years, he would be surer of success if he pledged that in his next inaugural address he would fight for a woman suffrage amendment. Arthur replied rather vaguely that he thought women ought to secure what they sought, but made no promises.

March 11   Asked Congress to consent to the United States taking part in an international convention for the protection of industrial property signed at Paris in March, 1883. Congress consented a few days later.

March 12   Issued an Executive Order condemning any person found shipping dangerous explosives to foreign ports, and stated that such persons would be prosecuted under the Revised Statutes of the United States which regulated the shipment of explosives.

March 20   Approved an appropriation of $30,000 to be used for the erection of a statue of James A. Garfield in the city of Washington.

March 26   Sent a Special Message to Congress requesting an appropriation of $4,283,000 to be used for the construction of four new cruisers and four new gunboats along modern lines. Congress disregarded Arthur's appeal.

April 1   Asked Congress for a special appropriation of $100,000 to be used for the repair and maintenance of levees destroyed by floods in the lower part of the Mississippi River Valley.

April 9   Issued an Executive Order stating that the Federal government would construct an exhibition at the World's Industrial and Cotton Centennial to be held at New Orleans for the purpose of illustrating the government's functions and administrative faculties in time of peace, and its resources as a war power.

April 11   Asked Congress for a permanent annual appropriation of $1,500,000 to provide the necessary armament for coastal and other fortifications. Congress cut his request to $700,000, and Arthur signed this measure on July 5, 1884.

April 14   Sent to Congress for ratification a convention concluded between the United States, France, and twenty-four other nations for the protection of submarine cables.

April 18   Announced to Congress that the government of Siam was sending a special embassy to visit the United States, and requested an appropriation to defray the expenses of the embassy while in the country. He also announced an approaching international conference to be held in Washington for the purpose of fixing upon a meridian proper to be employed as a common zero of longitude and standard of time reckoning throughout the globe.

April 24   Informed Congress that the Italian government was threatening to confiscate the American College in Rome, and that he was conducting negotiations to avoid such an action.

April 29   Instructed the Armaments and Foundries Board to develop a plan of action for the construction of a modern navy. Although Congress was hesitant in providing the money for such an undertaking, it, nevertheless, looked with favor upon such a proposal.

May 12   Signed a renewal of the Extradition Treaty with Great Britain.

May 13   Appointed a Special Board to plan and develop the government's exhibit at the New Orleans Centennial Exhibition. Designated W.A. DeCaindry as Secretary-Chairman of the Board.

May 14   Requested an appropriation of $224,556 from Congress in order to relocate the monuments and markers along the boundary between the United States and Mexico as decided at a convention of the two countries on June 29, 1882.

May 15   Asked Congress to pass legislation concerned with the regulation of the liquor traffic in Siam when citizens of the United States engage in the importation or sale of liquors there.

May 20   Arthur's political strength rested upon the support of New York businessmen to whom his conservative and sensible administration had been pleasing. On this date a mass meeting of New York businessmen and politicians was held at Cooper Union to demand Arthur's nomination at the Republican Convention the next month. Speakers representing all wings of the Republican Party mounted the rostrum, all praising Arthur, and the meeting appeared to be a great success. However, this popularity did not last, as a brief but sharp panic toward the end of the month made the Arthur Administration less appealing to the business community. In addition die-hard "Stalwarts," and Independent Republicans were not happy with Arthur either. Nevertheless, his chances for the nomination was still relatively bright.

May 29   Recommended to Congress a special appropriation be made to reward the services of the Osette Indians who had rescued and cared for the crew of the American steamer *Umatilla,* which had been wrecked near the coast of Vancouver Island.

June 3-7   The Republican National Convention met at Chicago, and on the fourth ballot nominated James G. Blaine of Maine for President. John A. Logan was nominated for Vice-President Arthur had led on the first three ballots, but on the fourth, the Convention swung to Blaine. It was generally believed that the President's cause had been incompetently handled by his floor managers. Arthur received the news at the White House, and immediately telegraphed Blaine pledging his support.

June 9   Submitted to Congress an estimate amounting to $588,000 for the government exhibit at the World's Industrial and

Cotton Centennial Exposition. His accompanying letter stressed the urgency of a special appropriation so that the Board appointed for this purpose could accomplish its desired end.

June 28   Proposed to Congress the creation of a Bureau of Labor Statistics, and urged the lawmakers to pass legislation for that purpose as quickly as possible.

July 2   Vetoed the bill entitled "An Act for the Relief of Fitz John Porter." Arthur protested that the bill was either an invasion of the Executive's appointing power, or else it was advice to the Executive which was unnecessary. His veto was sustained and Porter, who had been court-martialed during the Civil War, was not restored to his old rank and placed upon the retired list until Grover Cleveland did so two years later.

July 5   Arthur proposed the buying of a Nicaraguan Land Concession for the purpose of constructing a canal. Both the House and the Senate began serious debate on this proposal which was ultimately doomed to failure several months later.

July 8-11   The Democratic National Convention meeting at Chicago nominated Grover Cleveland of New York for President, and and Thomas A. Hendricks of Indiana for Vice-President. Independent Republicans who had been alienated by the nomination of Blaine whom they associated with the "Stalwart" wing of the Party, backed the Democratic candidate. These were the "Mugwumps" led by Carl Schurz, George William Curtis, E.L. Godkin, and Charles F. Adams Jr.

July 16   Issued a Proclamation admonishing and warning all persons who entered or intended to enter the Oklahoma lands in the Indian Territory. He stated that he would use the military if necessary to remove any person or persons who enroached on the Indian Reserves.

July 18   Issued an Executive Order which stated that the names of all persons who had successfully passed their examination under the civil service rules, may remain on the register of persons eligible for appointment two years from the date of their respective registrations, unless sooner appointed.

July 19   Called upon the states to strictly enforce their quarantine regulations so as to prevent the spread of disease which was unduly prevalent as a result of increased immigration to the United States.

September 4   Secretary of the Treasury Charles J. Folger died at his home in Geneva, New York. Arthur appointed as his replacement the Postmaster General W.Q. Gresham, and to replace Gresham, Frank Hatton became the new Postmaster General. When Gresham died a few months later, Arthur appointed as the new Secretary of the Treasury, Hugh McCulloch of New York.

October 29   The campaign of 1884 degenerated into one of the most scurrilous in American political history. The "Mulligan Letters" (1876), illuminating Blaine's corrupt dealings during his service as Speaker of the House, were fully exploited by the Democrats. The Republicans in turn charged that Cleveland had fathered an illegitimate child in Buffalo, New York. The key state in the election was New York, where the Tammany machine led by John Kelly opposed Cleveland. On this day, Rev. Samuel D. Burchard, leader of a delegation of clergymen who called on Blaine in New York, referred to the Democrats as the party of "Rum, Romanism, and Rebellion." Blaine's failure to disavow the remark or to rebuke Burchard cost him many votes in the Irish-American stronghold of New York. In addition, Arthur did very little actual campaigning for Blaine in his home state.

November 4   Cleveland defeated Blaine by a vote of 4,911,017 to 4,848,334. His margin in the Electoral College was 219 to 182. The Democrats carried New York by only 1,149 votes and Blaine later said this cost him the election. Arthur was also blamed by Republicans for not bringing in enough votes for Blaine.

November 18   Arthur concluded a General Treaty of Trade Reciprocity with Spain, but the Senate refused to ratify it during the remainder of his term.

December 1   Delivered his Fourth Annual Message in Congress. It dealt
with trade reciprocity, reform of the electoral college and
national defense. On the same day, the United States and
Nicaragua signed a convention which gave the United States
a strip of land across Nicaragua from sea to sea for the
purpose of constructing a canal. In return, the United
States was to give Nicaragua a four and a half million dollar
loan, accept her as a joint partner in the canal, and promise
to give her one-third of all eventual net revenues. Although
Arthur strongly urged ratification of the Convention, he was
admonished by the press and public alike for his actions
since the Clayton-Bulwer Treaty (1850) with England had as
yet not been abrogated.

December 4   Signed a Reciprocity Treaty with the Dominican Republic
and urged the Senate to ratify it. The Senate declined to do so.

On this day, a group of New York Republican Party leaders
met with Arthur to try to persuade him to run for the Senate
seat being vacated in New York. The President was placed
in a difficult position, for although he would have liked the
seat, he could not with dignity conduct a contest for a subordinate office at this time. His attitude, however, did not
deter those who supported him, and they continued to work
for his election during the next several weeks.

December 16   Arthur pushed a button in Washington which set all the
machinery at the World's Industrial and Cotton Centen-
nial Exposition in New Orleans in motion, and officially
declared the Exposition open.

December 20   At the Dupont Circle in Washington, Arthur dedicated a
statue to Admiral Dupont. Senator Bayard gave the principal speech.

December 22   Advised the Congress that the Gun Foundry Board had completed its plans, and that the steel companies were ready to
produce samples of armor plate and submit their bids for the
naval contracts. The Congress took no further action, however, on the construction of a modern navy.

1885

January 3   Arthur indicated that he would not permit his name to go
before the Republican Caucus at Albany choosing a Sena-

torial candidate. Thereupon, the Caucus selected William M. Evarts, who was elected by the Legislature the next day.

January 5 Issued an Executive Order concerned with disarming the Cheyenne and Arapahoe Indians in the Indian Territory by force if necessary.

January 25 Sent to Congress the Second Annual Report of the Civil Service Commission. Again, he praised its efficiency. By this date fifty percent of all postal officials were included on the classified list, and seventy-five percent of all those engaged in the Customs Service had come under civil service classification.

January 27 Sent a Special Message to Congress in which he voiced his opposition to private pension bills. He felt that special legislation of this character would set a dangerous precedent.

January 29 Despite President Arthur's pleas, the Senate refused to ratify the Nicaraguan Canal Treaty. Arthur was extremely disappointed.

January 30 Authorized the sending of several military instructors to Korea after that country had requested the services of American military personnel.

January 31 Issued a Proclamation announcing that the treaty of Washington concluded with Great Britain in May, 1871 concerning fishing rights of Americans in Canadian waters would terminate as of July 1, 1885.

February 2 Authorized the sending of a delegate to the Third International Conference of the Red Cross to be held at Geneva, Switzerland in September, 1885.

February 3 Graciously accepted for the United States government the swords and military and civil testimonials that had belonged to Ulysses S. Grant. The bequest was made by Grant's wife Julia Dent Grant.

February 5 Accepted in the name of the United States a piece of land donated by the Japanese government for the establishment of an American legation in that country.

February 12 Transmitted to Congress a request from the board of management of the World's Industrial and Cotton Centennial
Exposition for an emergency appropriation to meet a deficit
in its accounts, and for authority to reopen the exhibition
during the winter of 1885-86. Arthur recommended that
Congress accede to the board's wishes.

February 22 Attended the dedication of the Washington Monument, and
gave a great banquet to celebrate that evening.

February 27 Appointed his brother-in-law Henry Haynsworth (a civilian)
to the rank of Quartermaster and Captain in the Army.
Arthur was criticized by the press for "fraternal favoritism."
It was his last appointment as President.

March 2 Signed an extradition treaty with the government of
Mexico.

March 3 Nominated Grant to be a General on the retired list of the
Army, with the full pay of such rank. On this day, Arthur
urged the new Congress to authorize the construction of
ten new vessels; two cruisers, and eight other smaller
craft.

March 4 Signed an Appropriation Bill of $1,895,000 for the construc-
tion of two cruisers and two gunboats. It was not all that
Arthur desired, but at least the public and the Congress
were beginning to see the necessity of a strong, modern Navy.

At eleven o-clock, Grover Cleveland was inaugurated the
twenty-second President of the United States. After the
ceremonies, he went to ex-Secretary of State Frelinghuysen's
home for lunch. After a few more days, he left Washington
never to return.

RETIREMENT

March 10 Returned to his home in New York City. He tried to resume
his law practice with his old partners, S.W. Knevals and
R.S. Ronsom. But he had never entirely recovered since
his Florida trip, and was not really in good health. As the
months went by he began to feel worse.

August 1-20 Made a trip to the Berkshires, but his health did not improve.

December 25   Spent Christmas Day at the home of his nephew, Arthur Masten, and amused himself by reading some Christmas poetry to the family group.

1886

January 4   Accepted the presidency of his college fraternity, Psi Upsilon, and of the reorganized New York Arcade Railway, precursor of the subway system. But, Arthur was failing now. His doctor prescribed a strict retirement.

February 7   Arthur's illness was diagnosed as Bright's disease. Shortly after that, a dangerous heart condition was discovered.

March 8   Drew his will, naming Charles E. Miller, Daniel G. Rollins, and Seth Barton French as executors. He was now hopelessly ill.

July 5   Left for New London, Connecticut where he spent most of the summer in a vain quest for health.

November 13   He designated Augustus St. Gaudens to make a bust for the Senate wing of the Capitol.

November 16   Instead of spending his time in bed, Arthur rose, dressed, and chatted for a long time with two of his sisters about experiences of their childhood. At the end of the day, he retired in excellent spirits. During the night, he suffered a cerebral hemorrhage, and by morning was unconscious and partly paralyzed.

November 17   After one day's time, Chester Alan Arthur died. His children and sisters were at the bedside. His body was taken to Albany, and was buried at the Rural Cemetery, there on November 22.

DOCUMENTS

INAUGURAL ADDRESS
September 22, 1881

In a somber mood, Congress assembled to listen to the new President's Inaugural Address. It was quite short, and full of platitudes.

For the fourth time in the history of the Republic its Chief Magistrate has been removed by death. All hearts are filled with grief and horror at the hideous crime which has darkened our land, and the memory of the murdered President, his protracted sufferings, his unyielding fortitude, the example and achievements of his life, and the pathos of his death will forever illumine the pages of our history.

For the fourth time the officer elected by the people and ordained by the Constitution to fill a vacancy so created is called to assume the Executive chair. The wisdom of our fathers, foreseeing even the most dire possibilities, made sure that the Government should never be imperiled because of the uncertainty of human life. Men may die, but the fabrics of our free institutions remain unshaken. No higher or more assuring proof could exist of the strength and permanence of popular government than the fact that though the chosen of the people be struck down his constitutional successor is peacefully installed without shock or strain except the sorrow which mourns the bereavement. All the noble aspirations of my lamented predecessor which found expression in his life, the measures devised and suggested during his brief Administration to correct abuses, to enforce economy, to advance prosperity, and to promote the general welfare, to insure domestic security and maintain friendly and honorable relations with the nations of the earth, will be garnered in the hearts of the people; and it will be my earnest endeavor to profit, and to see that the nation shall profit, by his example and experience.

Prosperity blesses our country. Our fiscal policy is fixed by law, is well grounded and generally approved. No threatening issue mars our foreign intercourse, and the wisdom, integrity, and thrift of our people may be trusted to continue undisturbed the present assured career of peace, tranquillity, and welfare. The gloom and anxiety which have enshrouded the country must make repose especially welcome now. No demand for speedy legislation has been heard; no adequate occasion is apparent for an unusual session of Congress. The Constitution defines the functions and powers of the executive as clearly as those of either of the other two departments of the Government, and he must answer for the just exercise of the discretion it permits and the performance of the duties it imposes. Summoned to these high duties and responsibilities and profoundly conscious of their magnitude and gravity, I assume the trust imposed by the Constitution, relying for aid on divine guidance and the virtue, patriotism, and intelligence of the American people.

FIRST ANNUAL MESSAGE
December 6, 1881

In this, his first Annual Message to Congress, Arthur stressed civil service reform, and dealt with a host of matters relating to foreign policy.

To the Senate and House of Representatives of the United States:

An appalling calamity has befallen the American people since their chosen representatives last met in the halls where you are now assembled. We might else recall with unalloyed content the rare prosperity with which throughout the year the nation has been blessed. Its harvests have been plenteous; its varied industries have thriven; the health of its people has been preserved; it has maintained with foreign governments the undisturbed relations of amity and peace. For these manifestations of His favor we owe to Him who holds our destiny in His hands the tribute of our grateful devotion.

To that mysterious exercise of His will which has taken from us the loved and illustrious citizen who was but lately the head of the nation we bow in sorrow and submission.

The memory of his exalted character, of his noble achievements, and of his patriotic life will be treasured forever as a sacred possession of the whole people.

The announcement of his death drew from foreign governments and peoples tributes of sympathy and sorrow which history will record as signal tokens of the kinship of nations and the federation of mankind.

The feeling of good will between our own Government and that of Great Britain was never more marked than at present. In recognition of this pleasing fact I directed, on the occasion of the late centennial celebration at Yorktown, that a salute be given to the British flag . . .

The questions growing out of the proposed interoceanic waterway across the Isthmus of Panama are of grave national importance. This Government has not been unmindful of the solemn obligations imposed upon it by its compact of 1846 with Colombia, as the independent and sovereign mistress of the territory crossed by the canal, and has sought to render them effective by fresh engagements with the Colombian Republic looking to their practical execution. The negotiations to this end, after they had reached what appeared to be a mutually satisfactory solution here, were met in Colombia by a disavowal of the powers which its envoy had assumed and by a proposal for renewed negotiation on a modified basis.

Meanwhile this Government learned that Colombia had proposed to the European powers to join in a guaranty of the neutrality of the proposed Panama canal—a guaranty which would be in direct contravention of our obligation as the sole guarantor of the integrity of Colombian territory and of the neutrality of the canal itself. My lamented predecessor felt it his duty to place before the European powers the reasons which make the prior guaranty of the United States indispensable, and for which the interjection of any foreign guaranty might be regarded as a superfluous and unfriendly act.

Foreseeing the probable reliance of the British Government on the provisions of the Clayton-Bulwer treaty of 1850 as affording room for a share in the guaranties which the United States covenanted with Colombia four years before, I have not hesitated to supplement the action of my predecessor by proposing to Her Majesty's Government the modification of that instrument and the abrogation of such clauses thereof as do not comport with the obligations of the United States toward Colombia or with the vital needs of the two friendly parties to the compact.

This Government sees with great concern the continuance of the hostile relations between Chile, Bolivia, and Peru. An early peace between these Republics is much to be desired, not only that they may themselves be spared further misery and bloodshed, but because their continued antagonism threatens consequences which are, in my judgment, dangerous to the interests of republican government on this continent and calculated to destroy the best elements of our free and peaceful civilization.

As in the present excited condition of popular feeling in these countries there has been serious misapprehension of the position of the United States, and as separate diplomatic intercourse with each through independent ministers is sometimes subject, owning to the want of prompt reciprocal communication, to temporary misunderstanding, I have deemed it judicivus at the present time to send a special envoy accredited to all and each of them, and furnished with general instructions which will, I trust, enable him to bring these powers into friendly relations. . . .

The accompanying report of the Secretary of War will make known to you the operations of that Department for the past year.

He suggests measures for promoting the efficiency of the Army without adding to the number of its officers, and recommends the legislation necessary to increase the number of enlisted men to 30,000, the maximum allowed by law.

This he deems necessary to maintain quietude on our ever-shifting frontier; to preserve peace and suppress disorder and marauding in new settlements; to protect settlers and their property against Indians, and Indians against the encroachments of intruders; and to enable peaceable immigrants to establish homes in the most remote parts of our country.

The Army is now necessarily scattered over such a vast extent of territory that whenever an outbreak occurs reenforcements must be hurried from many quarters, over great distances, and always at heavy cost for transportation of men, horses, wagons, and supplies.

I concur in the recommendations of the Secretary for increasing the Army to the strength of 30,000 enlisted men.

It appears by the Secretary's report that in the absence of disturbances on the frontier the troops have been actively employed in collecting the Indians hitherto hostile and locating them on their proper reservations; that Sitting Bull and his adherents are now prisoners at Fort Randall; that the Utes have been moved to their new reservation in Utah; that during the recent outbreak of the Apaches it was necessary to reenforce the garrisons in Arizona by troops withdrawn from New Mexico; and that some of the Apaches are now held prisoners for trial, while some have escaped, and the majority of the tribe are now on their reservation.

There is need of legislation to prevent intrustion upon the lands set apart for the Indians. A large military force, at great expense, is now required to patrol the boundary line between Kansas and the Indian Territory. The only punishment that can at present be inflicted is the forcible removal of the intruder and the imposition of a pecuniary fine, which in most cases it is impossible to collect. There should be a penalty by imprisonment in such cases. . .

I commend to your attention the suggestions contained in this report in regard to the condition of our fortifications, especially our coast defenses, and recommend an increase of the strength of the Engineer Battalion, by which the efficiency of our torpedo system would be improved.

I also call your attention to the remarks upon the improvement of the South Pass of the Mississippi River, the proposed free bridge over the Potomac River at Georgetown, the importance of completing at an early day the north wing of the War Department building, and other recommendations of the Secretary of War which appear in his report.

The actual expenditures of that Department for the fiscal year ending Une 30, 1881, were $42,122,201.39. The appropriations for the year 1882 were $44,889,725.42. The estimates for 1883 are $44,541,276.91.

The report of the Secretary of the Navy exhibits the condition of that branch of the service and presents valuable suggestions for its improvement. I call your especial attention also to the appended report of the Advisory Board which he convened to devise suitable measures for increasing the efficiency of the Navy, and particularly to report as to the character and number of vessels necessary to place it upon a footing commensurate with the necessities of the Government.

I can not too strongly urge upon you my conviction that every consideration of national safety, economy, and honor imperatively demands a thorough rehabilitation of our Navy . . .

In my letter accepting the nomination for the Vice-Presidency I stated that
in my judgment—

> No man should be the incumbent of an office the duties of which
> he is for any cause unfit to perform; who is lacking in the ability
> fidelity, or integrity which a proper administration of such office
> demands. This sentiment would doubtless meet with general
> acquiescence, but opinion has been widely divided upon the
> wisdom and practicability of the various reformatory schemes
> which have been suggested and of certain proposed regulations
> governing appointments to public office.
>
> The efficiency of such regulations has been distrusted mainly
> because they have seemed to exalt mere educational and abstract
> tests above general business capacity and even special fitness for the
> particular work in hand. It seems to me that the rules which should
> be applied to the management of the public service may properly
> conform in the main to such as regulate the conduct of successful
> private business:
>
> Original appointments should be based upon ascertained fitness.
>
> The tenure of office should be stable.
>
> Positions of responsibility should, so far as practicable, be filled
> by the promotion of worthy and efficient officers.
>
> The investigation of all complaints and the punishment of all
> official misconduct should be prompt and thorough.

The views expressed in the foregoing letter are those which will govern
my administration of the executive office. They are doubtless shared by
all intelligent and patriotic citizens, however divergent in their opinions
as to the best methods of putting them into practical operation.

For example, the assertion that "original appointments should be based
upon ascertained fitness" is not open to dispute.

But the question how in practice such fitness can be most effectually
ascertained is one which has for years excited interest and discussion. The
measure which, with slight variations in its details, has lately been urged
upon the attention of Congress and the Executive has as its principal
feature the scheme of competitive examination. Save for certain exceptions,
which need not here be specified, this plan would allow admission to the
service only in its lowest grade, and would accordingly demand that all
vacancies in higher positions should be filled by promotion alone. In these
particulars it is in conformity with the existing civil-service system of Great
Britain; and indeed the success which has attended that system in the
country of its birth is the strongest argument which has been urged for its
adoption here.

The fact should not, however, be overlooked that there are certain
features of the English system which have not generally been received with

favor in this country, even among the foremost advocates of civil-service reform.

Among them are:

1. A tenure of office which is substantially a life tenure.

2. A limitation of the maximum age at which an applicant can enter the service, whereby all men in middle life or older are, with some exceptions, rigidly excluded.

3. A retiring allowance upon going out of office.

These three elements are as important factors of the problem as any of the others. To eliminate them from the English system would effect a most radical change in its theory and practice.

The avowed purpose of that system is to induce the educated young men of the country to devote their lives to public employment by an assurance that having once entered upon it they need never leave it, and that after voluntary retirement they shall be the recipients of an annual pension. That this system as an entirety has proved very successful in Great Britain seems to be generally conceded even by those who once opposed its adoption.

To a statute which should incorporate all its essential features I should feel bound to give my approval; but whether it would be for the best interests of the public to fix upon an expedient for immediate and extensive application which embraces certain features of the English system, but excludes or ignores others of equal importance, may be seriously doubted, even by those who are impressed, as I am myself, with the grave importance of correcting the evils which inhere in the present methods of appointment.

If, for example, the English rule which shuts out persons about the age of 25 years from a large number of public employments is not to be made an essential part of our own system, it is questionable whether the attainment of the highest number of marks at a competitive examination should be the criterion by which all applications should be put to test. And under similar conditions it may also be questioned whether admission to the service should be strictly limited to its lowest ranks.

There are very many characteristcs which go to make a model civil servant. Prominent among them are probity, industry, good sense, good habits, good temper, patience, order, courtesy, tact, self-reliance, manly deference to superior officers, and manly consideration for inferiors. The absence of these traits is not supplied by wide knowledge of books, or by promptitude in answering questions, or by any other quality likely to be brought to light by competitive examination.

To make success in such a contest, therefore, an indispensable condition of public employment would very likely result in the practical exclusion of the older applicants, even though they might possess qualifications far superior to their younger and more brilliant competitors.

These suggestions must not be regarded as evincing any spirit of opposition to the competitive plan, which has been to some extent successfully employed already, and which may hereafter vindicate the claim of its most earnest supporters; but it ought to be seriously considered whether the application of the same educational standard to persons of mature years and to young men fresh from school and college would not be likely to exalt mere intellectual proficiency above other qualitites of equal or greater importance.

Another feature of the proposed system is the selection by promotion of all officers of the Government above the lowest grade, except such as would fairly be regarded as exponents of the policy of the Executive and the principles of the dominant party.

To afford encouragement to faithful public servants by exciting in their minds the hope of promotion if they are found to merit it is much to be desired.

But would it be wise to adopt a rule so rigid as to permit no other mode of supplying the intermediate walks of the service?

There are many persons who fill subordinate positions with great credit, but lack those qualities which are requisite for higher posts of duty; and, besides, the modes of thought and action of one whose ervice in a governmental bureau has been long continued are often so cramped by routine procedure as almost to disqualify him from instituting changes required by the public interests. An infusion of new blood from time to time into the middle ranks of the service might be very beneficial in its results.

The subject under discussion is one of grave importance. The evils which are complained of can not be eradicated at once; the work must be gradual. . .

I can not doubt that these important questions will receive your early and thoughtful consideration.

Deeply impressed with the gravity of the responsibilities which have so unexpectedly devolved upon me, it will be my constant purpose to cooperate with you in such measures as will promote the glory of the country and the prosperity of its people.

VETO OF CHINESE EXCLUSION ACT
April 4, 1882

When Congress attempted to pass a Chinese Exclusion Act in violation of the Burlingame Treaty of 1868, President Arthur vetoed the measure.

To the Senate of the United States:

After careful consideration of Senate bill No. 71, entitled "An act to execute certain treaty stipulations relating to Chinese," I herewith return it to the Senate, in which it originated, with my objections to its passage.

A nation is justified in repudiating its treaty obligations only when they are in conflict with great paramount interests. Even then all possible reasonable means for modifying or changing those obligations by mutual agreement should be exhausted before resorting to the supreme right of refusal to comply with them.

These rules have governed the United States in their past intercourse with other powers as one of the family of nations. I am persuaded that if Congress can feel that this act violates the faith of the nations as pledged to China it will concur with me in rejecting this particular mode of regulating Chinese immigration, and will endeavor to find another which shall meet the expectations of the people of the United States without coming in conflict with the rights of China.

The present treaty relations between that power and the United States spring from an antagonism which arose between our paramount domestic interests and our previous relations.

The treaty commonly known as the Burlingame treaty conferred upon Chinese subjects the right of voluntary emigration to the United States for the purposes of curiosity or trade or as permanent residents, and was in all respects reciprocal as to citizens of the United States in China. It gave to the voluntary emigrant coming to the United States the right to travel there or to reside there, with all the privileges, immunities, or exemptions enjoyed by the citizens or subjects of the most favored nation.

Under the operation of this treaty it was found that the institutions of the United States and the character of its people and their means of obtaining a livelihood might be seriously affected by the unrestricted introduction of Chinese labor. Congress attempted to alleviate this condition by legislation, but the act which it passed proved to be in violation of our treaty obligations, and, being returned by the President with his objections, failed to become a law.

Diplomatic relief was then sought. A new treaty was concluded with China. Without abrogating the Burlingame treaty, it was agreed to modify it so far that the Government of the United States might regulate, limit, or suspend the coming of Chinese laborers to the United States or their residence therein, but that it should not absolutely prohibit them, and that the limitation or suspension should be reasonable and should apply only to Chinese who might go to the United States as laborers, other classes not being included in the limitations. This treaty is unilateral, not reciprocal. It is a concession from China to the United States in limitation of the rights which she was enjoying under the Burlingame treaty. It leaves us by our own act to determine when and how we will enforce those limitations. China may therefore fairly have a right to expect that in enforcing them we will take good care not to overstep the grant and take more than has been conceded to us.

It is but a year since this new treaty, under the operation of the Constitution, became part of the supreme law of the land, and the present act is the first attempt to exercise the more enlarged powers which it relinquishes to the United States. . .

The examination which I have made of the treaty and of the declarations which its negotiators have left on record of the meaning of its language leaves no doubt in my mind that neither contracting party in concluding the treaty of 1880 contemplated the passage of an act prohibiting immigration for twenty years, which is nearly a generation, or thought that such a period would be a reasonable suspension or limitation, or intended to change the provisions of the Burlingame treaty to that extent. I regard this provision of the act as a breach of our national faith, and being unable to bring myself in harmony with the views of Congress on this vital point the honor of the country constrains me to return the act with this objection to its passage.

Deeply convinced of the necessity of some legislation on this subject, and concurring fully with Congress in many of the objects which are sought to be accomplished, I avail myself of the opportunity to point out some other features of the present act which, in my opinion, can be modified to advantage.

The classes of Chinese who still enjoy the protection of the Burlingame treaty are entitled to the privileges, immunities, and exemptions accorded to citizens and subjects of the most favored nation. We have treaties with many powers which permit their citizens and subjects to reside within the Sunited States and carry on business under the same laws and regulations which are enforced against citizens of the United Stats. I think it may be doubted whether provisions requiring personal registration and the taking out of passports which are not imposed upon natives can be required of Chinese. Without expressing an opinion on that point, I may invite the attention of Congress to the fact that the system of personal registration and passports is undemocratic and hostile to the spirit of our institutions. I doubt the wisdom of putting an entering wedge of this kind into our laws.

A nation like the United States, jealous of the liberties of its citizens, may well hesitate before it incorporates into its policy a system which is fast disappearing in Europe before the progress of liberal institutions. A wide experience has shown how futile such precautions are, and how easily passports may be borrowed, exchanged, or even forged by persons interested to do so.

If it is, nevertheless, thought that a passport is the most convenient way for identifying the Chinese entitled to the protection of the Burlingame treaty, it may still be doubted whether they ought to be required to register. It is certainly our duty under the Burlingame treaty to make their stay in the United States, in the operation of general laws upon them, as nearly like that of our own citizens as we can consistently with our right to shut out the laborers. No good purpose is served in requiring them to register.

My attention has been called by the Chinese minister to the fact that the bill as it stands makes no provision for the transit across the United States of Chinese subjects now residing in foreign countries. I think that this point may well claim the attention of Congress in legislating on this subject.

I have said that good faith requires us to suspend the immigration of Chinese laborers for a less period than twenty years; I now add that good policy points in the same direction. . .

ON THE MISSISSIPPI RIVER COMMISSION
April 17, 1882

Due to disastrous floods in the Mississippi River Valley, Arthur recommended special appropriations to help the people of that region.

To the Senate and House of Representatives:

I transmit herewith a letter, dated the 29th ultimo, from the Secretary of War, inclosing copy of a communication from the Mississippi River Commission, in which the commission recommends that an appropriation may be made of $1,010,000 for "closing existing gaps in levees," in addition to the like sum for which an estimate has already been submitted.

The subject is one of such importance that I deem it proper to recommend early and favorable consideration of the recommendations of the commission. Having possession of and jurisdiction over the river, Congress, with a view of improving its navigation and protecting the people of the valley from floods, has for years caused surveys of the river to be made for the purpose of acquiring knowledge of the laws that control it and of its phenomena. By act approved June 28, 1879, the Mississippi River Commission was created, composed of able engineers. Section 4 of the act provides that—

> It shall be the duty of said commission to take into consideration and mature such plan or plans and estimates as will correct, permanently locate, and deepen the channel and protect the banks of the Mississippi River; improve and give safety and east to the navigation thereof; prevent destructive floods; promote and facilitate commerce, trade, and the postal service.

The constitutionality of a law making appropriations in aid of these objects can not be questioned. While the report of the commission submitted and the plans proposed for the river's improvement seem justified as well on scientific principles as by experience and the approval of the people most interested, I desire to leave it to the judgment of Congress to decide upon the best plan for the permanent and complete improvement of the navigation of the river and for the protection of the valley.

The immense losses and widespread suffering of the people dwelling near the river induce me to urge upon Congress the propriety of not only making an appropriation to close the gaps in the levees occasioned by the recent floods, as recommended by the commission, but that Congress should inaugurate measures for the permanent improvement of the navigation of the river and security of the valley. It may be that such a system of improvement would as it progressed require the appropriation of twenty or thirty millions of dollars. Even such an expenditure, extending, as it must, over several years, can not be regarded as extravagant in view of the immense interest involved. The safe and convenient navigation of the Mississippi is a matter of concern to all sections of the country, but to the Northwest, with its immense harvests, needing cheap transportation to the sea, and to the inhabitants of the river valley, whose lives and property depend upon the proper construction of the safeguards which protect from from the floods, it is of vital importance that a well-matured and comprehensive plan for improvement should be put into operation with as little delay as possible. The cotton product of the region subject to the devastating floods is a source of wealth to the nation and of great importance to keeping the balances of trade in our favor.

It may not be inopportune to mention that this Government has imposed and collected some $70,000,000 by a tax on cotton, in the production of which the population of the Lower Mississippi is largely engaged, and it does not seem inequitable to return a portion of this tax to those who contributed it, particularly as such an action will also result in an important gain to the country at large, and especially so to the great and rich States of the Northwest and the Mississippi Valley.

ON LAWLESSNESS IN THE TERRITORY OF ARIZONA
April 26, 1882

*In a Special Message to Congress, Arthur angrily discussed
violence and disrespect for the law in one of the last areas of the
"wild west."*

To the Senate and House of Representatives:

By recent information received from official and other sources I am
advised that an alarming state of disorder continues to exist within the
Territory of Arizona, and that lawlessness has already gained such head
there as to require a resort to extraordinary means to repress it.

The governor of the Territory, under date of the 31st ultimo, reports
that violence and anarchy prevail, particularly in Cochise County and
along the Mexican border; that robbery, murder, and resistance to law
have become so common as to cease causing surprise, and that the people
are greatly intimidated and losing confidence in the protection of the law.
I transmit his communication herewith and call special attention thereto.

In a telegram from the General of the Army dated at Tucson, Ariz., on
the 11th instant, herewith transmitted, that officer states that he hears of
lawlessness and disorders which seem well attested, and that the civil
officers have not sufficient force to make arrests and hold the prisoners
for trial or punish them when convicted.

Much of this disorder is caused by armed bands of desperadoes known
as "Cowboys," by whom depredations are not only committed within the
Territory, but it is alleged predatory incursions are made therefrom into
Mexico. In my message to Congress at the beginning of the present session
I called attention to the existence of these bands and suggested that the
setting on foot without our own territory of brigandage and armed marauding expeditions against friendly nations and their citizens be made punish-
able as an offense against the United States. I renew this suggestion.

To effectually repress the lawlessness prevailing within the Territory a
prompt execution of the process of the courts and vigorous enforcement
of the laws against offenders are needed. This the civil authorities there
are unable to do without the aid of other means and forces than they can
now avail themselves of. To meet the present exigencies the governor asks
that provision be made by Congress to enable him to employ and maintain
temporarily a volunteer militia force to aid the civil authorities, the members of which force to be invested with the same powers and authority as are
conferred by the laws of the Territory upon peace officers thereof.

On the ground of economy as well as effectiveness, however, it appears
to me to be more advisable to permit the cooperation with the civil authorities of a part of the Army as a *posse comitatus.* Believing that this, in addition

to such use of the Army as may be made under the powers already conferred by section 5298, Revised Statutes, would be adequate to secure the accomplishment of the ends in view, I again call the attention of Congress to the expediency of so amending section 15 of the act of June 18, 1878, chapter 263, as to allow the military forces to be employed as a *posse comitatus* to assist the civil authorities within a Territory to execute the laws therein. This use of the Army, as I have in my former message observed, would not seem to be within the alleged evil against which that legislation was aimed.

VETO OF AN IMMIGRATION ACT
July 1, 1882

*Another Act designed by Congress to limit immigration to the
United States was sharply denounced by Arthur who vetoed
the measure.*

To the House of Representatives of the United States:

Herewith I return House bill No. 2744, entitled "An act to regulate the
carriage of passengers by sea," without my approval. In doing this I regret
that I am not able to give my assent to an act which has received the sanction
of the majority of both Houses of Congress.

The object proposed to be secured by the act is meritorious and philan-
thropic. Some correct and accurate legislation upon this subject is undoubtedly necessary. Steamships that bring large bodies of emigrants must
be subjected to strict legal enactments, so as to prevent the passengers from
being exposed to hardship and suffering; and such legislation should be
made as will give them abundance of space and air and light, protecting their
health by affording all reasonable comforts and conveniences and by providing for the quantity and quality of the food to be furnished and all of the
other essentials of roomy, safe, and healthful accommodations in their
passage across the sea.

A statute providing for all this is absolutely needed, and in the spirit of
humane legislation must be enacted. The present act, by most of its provisions, will obtain and secure this protection for such passengers, and were
it not for some serious errors contained in it it would be most willingly
approved by me.

My objections are these: In the first section, in lines from 13 to 24, inclusive, it is provided "that the compartments or spaces," etc., "shall be of
sufficient dimensions to allow for each and any passenger," etc., "100 cubic
feet, if the compartment or space is located on the first deck next below
the uppermost deck of the vessel," etc., "or 120 cubic feet for each passenger," etc., "if the compartment or space is located on the second deck below
the uppermost deck of the vessel," etc. "It shall not be lawful to carry or
bring passengers on any deck other than the two decks mentioned," etc.

Nearly all of the new and most of the improved ocean steamers have a
spar deck, which is above the main deck. The main deck was in the old style
of steamers the only uppermost deck. The spar deck is a comparatively new
feature of the large and costly steamships, and is now practically the uppermost deck. Below this spar deck is the main deck. Because of the misuse of
the words "uppermost deck" instead of the use of the words "main deck" by
this act, the result will be to exclude nearly all of the large steamships from
carrying passengers anywhere but on the main deck and on the deck below,

which is the steerage deck, and to leave the orlop, or lower deck, heretofore used for passengers, useless and unoccupied by passengers. This objection, which is now presented in connection with others that will be presently explained, will, if this act is enforced as it is now phrased, render useless for passenger traffic and expose to heavy loss all of the great ocean steam lines; and it will also hinder emigration, as there will not be ships enough that could accept these conditions to carry all who may wish to come.

The use of the new and the hitherto unknown term "uppermost deck" creates this difficulty, and I can not consent to have an abuse of terms like this to operate thus injuriously to these large fleets of ships. The passengers will not be benefited by such a statute, but emigration will be hindered, if not for a while almost prevented for many.

Again, the act in the first section, from line 31 to line 35, inclusive, provides: "And such passengers shall not be carried or brought in any between-decks, nor in any compartment," etc., "the clear height of which is less than 7 feet." Between the decks of all ships are the beams; they are about a foot in width. The legal method of ascertaining tonnage for the purpose of taxation is to measure between the beams from the floor to the ceiling. If this becomes a law the space required would be 8 feet from floor to ceiling, and this is impracticable, for in all ships the spaces between decks are adjusted in proportion to the dimensions of the ship; and if these spaces between decks are changed so as not to correspond in their proportions with the dimensions of the vessel, the ship will not work well in the sea, her sailing qualities will be injured, and she will be rendered unfit for service.

It is only in great ships of vast tonnage that the height between decks can be increased. All the ordinary-sized ships are necessarily constructed with 7 feet space in the interval between the beams from the floor to the ceiling. To adopt this act, with this provision, would be to drive out of the service of transporting passengers most all of the steamships now insuch trade, and no practical good obtained by it, for really, with the exception of the narrow beam, the space between the decks is now 7 feet. The purpose of the space commanded by the act is to obtain sufficient air and ventilation, and that is actually now given to the passenger by the 7 feet that exists in all of these vessels between floor and ceiling.

There is also another objection that I must suggest. In section 12, from line 14 to line 24, it is provided: "Before such vessel shall be cleared or may lawfully depart," etc., "the master of said vessel shall furnish," etc., "a correct list of all passengers who have been or are intended to be taken on board the vessel, and shall specify," etc. This provision would prevent the clearing of the vessel. Steam vessels start at an appointed hour and with punctuality. Down almost to the very hour of their departure new passengers, other than those who have engaged their passage, constantly come on board.If this provision is to be the law, they must be rejected, for the ship can not, without incurring heavy penalties, take passengers whose names are not set forth on the list required before such vessel shall be cleared. They should be allowed to take such new passengers upon condition that they would furnish an additional list containing such persons' names. There are other points of objection of a minor character that might be presented for consideration if the bill could be reconsidered and amended, but the three that I have recited are conspicuous defects in a bill that ought to be a code for such a purpose, clear and explicit, free from all such objections. The practical result of this law would be to subject all of the competing lines of large ocean steamers to great losses. By restricting their carrying accommodations it would also stay the current of emigration that it is our policy to encourage as well as to protect. A good bill, correctly phrased, and expressing and naming in plain, well-known technical terms the proper and usual places and decks where passengers are and ought to be placed and carried, will receive my prompt and immediate assent as a public necessity and blessing.

VETO OF THE RIVERS AND HARBORS ACT
August 1, 1882

Congress attempted to pass a $19,000,000 Rivers and Harbors Act, which President Arthur labeled a "pork barrel" measure, and promptly vetoed.

To the House of Representatives:

Having watched with much interest the progress of House bill No. 6242, entitled "An act making appropriations for the construction, repair, and preservation of certain works on rivers and harbors, and for other purposes," and having since it was received carefully examined it, after mature consideration I am constrained to return it herewith to the House of Representatives, in which it originated, without my signature and with my objections to its passage.

Many of the appropriations in the bill are clearly for the general welfare and most beneficial in their character. Two of the objects for which provision is made were by me considered so important that I felt it my duty to direct to them the attention of Congress. In my annual message in December last I urged the vital importance of legislation for the reclamation of the marshes and for the establishment of the harbor lines along the Potomac front. In April last, by special message, I recommended an appropriation for the improvement of the Mississippi River. It is not necessary that I say that when my signature would make the bill appropriating for these and other valuable national objects a law it is with great reluctance and only under a sense of duty that I withhold it.

My principle objection to the bill is that it contains appropriations for purposes not for the common defense or general welfare, and which do not promote commerce among the States. These provisions, on the contrary, are entirely for the benefit of the particular localities in which it is proposed to make the improvements. I regard such appropriation of the public money as beyond the powers given by the Constitution to Congress and the President.

I feel the more bound to withhold my signature from the bill because of the peculiar evils which manifestly result from this infraction of the Constitution. Appropriations of this nature, to be devoted purely to local objects, tend to an increase in number and in amount. As the citizens of one State find that money, to raise which they in common with the whole country are taxed, is to be expended for local imprvements in another State, they demand similar benefits for themselves, and it is not unnatural that they should seek to indemnify themselves for such use of the public funds by securing appropriations for similar improvements in their own neighborhood. Thus as the bill becomes more objectionable it secures more support.

This result is invariable and necessarily follows a neglect to observe the constitutional limitations imposed upon the lawmaking power. . .

While feeling every dispostion to leave to the Legislature the responsibility of determining what amount should be appropriated for the purposes of the bill, so long as the appropriations are confined to objects indicated by the grant of power, I can not escape the conclusion that, as a part of the lawmaking power of the Government, the duty devolves upon me to withhold my signature from a bill containing appropriations which in my opinion greatly exceed in amount the needs of the country for the present fiscal year. It being the usage to provide money for these purposes by annual appropriation bills, the President is in effect directed to expend so large an amount of money within so brief a period that the expenditure can not be made economically and advantageously. . .

SECOND ANNUAL MESSAGE
December 4, 1882

In a very long message to Congress, Arthur again discussed in detail American foreign affairs, and Indian troubles. Once more he made a special plea for civil service reform, and defense appropriations.

To the Senate and House of Representatives of the United States:

It is provided by the Constitution that the President shall from time to time give to the Congress information of the state of the Union and recommend to their consideration such measures as he shall judge necessary and expedient.

In reviewing the events of the year which has elapsed since the commencement of your sessions, I first call your attention to the gratifying condition of our foreign affairs. Our intercourse with other powers has continued to be of the most friendly character.

Such slight differences as have arisen during the year have already been settled or are likely to reach an early adjustment. The arrest of citizens of the United States in Ireland under recent laws which owe their origin to the disturbed condition of that country has led to a somewhat extended correspondence with the Government of Great Britain. A disposition to respect our rights has been partially manifested by the release of the arrested parties.

The claim of this nation in regard to the supervision and control of any interoceanic canal across the American Isthmus has continued to be the subject of conference.

It is likely that time will be more powerful than discussion in removing the divergence between the two nations whose friendship is so closely cemented by the intimacy of their relations and the community of their interests.

Our long-established friendliness with Russia has remained unshaken. It has prompted me to proffer the earnest counsels of this Government that measures be adopted for suppressing the proscription which the Hebrew race in that country has lately suffered. It has not transpired that any American citizen has been subjected to arrest or injury, but our courteous remonstrance has nevertheless been courteously received. There is reason to believe that the time is not far distant when Russia will be able to secure toleration to all faiths within her borders. . .

The war between Peru and Bolivia on the one side and Chile on the other began more than three years ago. On the occupation by Chile in 1880 of all the littoral territory of Bolivia, negotiations for peace were conducted under the direction of the United States. The allies refused to concede any territory, but Chile has since become master of the whole coast of both countries and of the capital of Peru. A year since, as you have already been advised by correspondence transmitted to you in January last, this Government sent a special mission to the belligerent powers to express the hope that Chile would be disposed to accept a money indemnity for the expenses of the war and to relinquish her demand for a portion of the territory of her antagonist.

This recommendation, which Chile declined to follow, this Government did not assume to enforce; nor can it be enforced without resort to measures which would be in keeping neither with the temper of our people nor with the spirit of our institutions.

The power of Peru no longer extends over its whole territory, and in the event of our interference to dictate peace would need to be supplemented by the armies and navies of the United States. Such interference would almost inevitably lead to the establishment of a protectorate—a result utterly at odds with our past policy, injurious to our present interests, and full of embarrassments for the future.

For effecting the termination of hostilities upon terms at once just to the victorious nation and generous to its adversaries, this Government has spared no efforts save such as might involve the complications which I have indicated.

It is greatly to be deplored that Chile seems resolved to exact such rigorous conditions of peace and indisposed to submit to arbitration the terms of an amicable settlement. No peace is likely to be lasting that is not sufficiently equitable and just to command the approval of other nations.

About a year since invitations were extended to the nations of this continent to send representatives to a peace congress to assemble at Washington in November, 1882. The time of meeting was fixed at a period then remote, in the hope, as the invitation itself declared, that in the meantime the disturbances between the South American Republics would be adjusted. As that expectation seemed unlikely to be realized, I asked in April last year for an expression of opinion from the two Houses of Congress as to the advisability of holding the proposed convention at the time appointed. This action was prompted in part by doubts which mature reflection had suggested whether the diplomatic usage and traditions of the Government did not make it fitting that the Executive should consult the representatives of the people before pursuing a line of policy somewhat novel in its character and far reaching in its possible consequences. In view of the fact that no action was taken by Congress in the premises and that no provision had been made for necessary expenses, I subsequently decided to postpone the convocation, and so notified the several Governments which had been invited to attend.

I am unwilling to dismiss this subject without assuring you of my support of any measures the wisdom of Congress may devise for the promotion of peace on this continent and throughout the world, and I trust that the time is nigh when, with the universal assent of civilized peoples, all international differences shall be determined without resort to arms by the benignant processes of arbitration. . .

I renew my recommendation of such legislation as will place the United States in harmony with other maritime powers with respect to the international rules for the prevention of collisions at sea.

In conformity with your joint resolution of the 3d of August last, I have directed the Secretary of State to address foreign governments in respect to a proposed conference for considering the subject of the universal adoption of a common prime meridian to be used in the reckoning of longitude and in the regulation of time throughout the civilized world. Their replies will in due time be laid before you.

An agreement was reached at Paris in 1875 between the principal powers for the interchange of official publications through the medium of their respective foreign departments. . . .

It is a momentous question for the decision of Congress whether immediate and substantial aid should not be extended by the General Government for supplementing the efforts of private beneficence and of State and Territorial legislation in behalf of education.

The regulation of interstate commerce has already been the subject of your deliberations. One of the incidents of the marvelous extension of the railway system of the country has been the adoption of such measures by the corporations which own or control the roads as have tended to impair the advantages of healthful competition and to make hurtful discriminations in the adjustment of freightage.

These inequalities have been corrected in several of the States by appropriate legislation, the effect of which is necessarily restricted to the limits of their own territory.

So far as such mischiefs affect commerce between the States or between any one of the States and a foreign country, they are subjects of national concern, and Congress alone can afford relief. . .

The communication which I made to Congress at its first session, in December last, contained a somewhat full statement of my sentiments in relation to the principles and rules which ought to govern appointments to public service.

Referring to the various plans which had theretofore been the subject of discussion in the National Legislature (plans which in the main were modeled upon the system which obtains in Great Britain, but which lacked certain of the prominent features whereby that system is distinguished),

I felt bound to intimate by doubts whether they, or any of them, would afford adequate remedy for the evils which they aimed to correct.

I declared, nevertheless, that if the proposed measures should prove acceptable to Congress they would receive the unhesitating support of the Executive.

Since these suggestions were submitted for your consideration there has been no legislation upon the subject to which they relate, but there has meanwhile been an increase in the public interest in that subject, and the people of the country, apparently without distinction of party, have in various ways and upon frequent occasions given expression to their earnest wish for prompt and definite action. In my judgment such action should no longer be postponed.

I may add that my own sense of its pressing importance has been quickened by observation of a practical phase of the matter, to which attention has more than once been called by my predecessors.

The civil list now comprises about 100,000 persons, far the larger part of whom must, under the terms of the Constitution, be selected by the President either directly or through his own appointees.

In the early years of the administration of the Government the personal direction of appointments to the civil service may not have been an irksome task for the Executive, but now that the burden has increased fully a hundredfold it has become greater than he ought to bear, and it necessarily diverts his time and attention from the proper discharge of other duties no less delicate and responsible, and which in the very nature of things can not be delegated to other hands.

In the judgment of not a few who have given study and reflection to this matter, the nation has outgrown the provisions which the Constitution has established for filling the minor offices in the public service.

But whatever may be thought of the wisdom or expediency of changing the fundamental law in this regard, it is certain that much relief may be afforded, not only to the President and to the heads of the Departments, but to Senators and Representatives in Congress, by discreet legislation. They would be protected in a great measure by the bill now pending before the Senate, or by any other which should embody its important features, from the pressure of personal importunity and from the labor of examining conflicting claims and pretensions of candidates. . . .

In July last I authorized a public announcement that employees of the Government should regard themselves as at liberty to exercise their pleasure in making or refusing to make political contributions, and that their action in that regard would in no manner affect their official status.

In this announcement I acted upon the view, which I had always maintained and still maintain, that a public officer should be as absolutely free as any other citizen to give or to withhold a contribution for the aid of the political party of his choice. It has, however, been urged, and doubtless not without foundation in fact, that by solicitation of official superiors and by other modes such contributions have at times been obtained from persons whose only motive for giving has been the fear of what might befall them if they refused. It goes without saying that such contributions are not voluntary, and in my judgment their collection should be prohibited by law. A bill which will effectually suppress them will receive my cordial approval. . .

Among the questions which have been the topic of recent debate in the halls of Congress none are of greater gravity than those relating to the ascertainment of the vote for Presidential electors and the intendment of the Constitution in its provisions for devolving Executive functions upon the Vice-President when the President suffers from inability to discharge the powers and duties of his office.

I trust that no embarrassments may result from a failure to determine these questions before another national election. . .

ON THE APPOINTMENT OF A CHIEF EXAMINER
FOR THE CIVIL SERVICE COMMISSION
March 1, 1883

In accordance with the provisions of the Pendleton Act passed January 16, 1883, President Arthur appoined a Chief-Examiner of the Civil Service Commission.

To the Senate of the United States:

Having approved the act recently passed by Congress "to regulate and improve the civil service of the United States," I deem it my duty to call your attention to the provision for the employment of a "chief examiner" contained in the third section of the act, which was the subject of consideration at the time of its approval.

I am advised by the Attorney-General that there is great doubt whether such examiner is not properly an officer of the United States because of the nature of his employment, its duration, emolument, and duties. If he be such, the provision for his employment (which involves an appointment by the Commission) is not in conformity with section 2, Article II of the Constitution. Assuming this to be the case, the result would be that the appointment of the chief examiner must be deemed to be vested in the President, by and with the advice and consent of the Senate, since in such case the appointment would not be otherwise provided for by law. Concurring in this opinion, I nominate Silas W. Burt, of New York, to be chief examiner of the Civil Service Commission.

CHESTER A. ARTHUR

THIRD ANNUAL MESSAGE
December 4, 1883

Arthur devoted a large part of this State of the Union Address to national defense, especially to the development of a modern, steel navy. Some results would be forthcoming during the following year.

To the Congress of the United States:

At the threshold of your deliberations I congratulate you upon the favorable aspect of the domestic and foreign affairs of this Government.

Our relations with other countries continue to be upon a friendly footing. With the Argentine Republic, Austria, Belgium, Brazil, Denmark, Hayti, Italy, Santo Domingo, and Sweden and Norway no incident has occurred which calls for special comment. The recent opening of new lines of telegraphic communication with Central America and Brazil permitted the interchange of messages of friendship with the Governments of those countries.

During the year there have been perfected and proclaimed consular and commercial treaties with Servia and a consular treaty with Roumania, thus extending our intercourse with the Danubian countries, while our Eastern relations have been put upon a wider basis by treaties with Korea and Madagascar. The new boundary-survey treaty with Mexico, a trade-marks convention and a supplementary treaty of extradition with Spain, and conventions extending the duration of the Franco-American Claims Commission have also been proclaimed.

Notice of the termination of the fisheries articles of the treaty of Washington was duly given to the British Government, and the reciprocal privileges and exemptions of the treaty will accordingly cease on July 1, 1885. The fisheries industries, pursued by a numerous class of our citizens on the northern coasts, both of the Atlantic and Pacific oceans, are worthy of the fostering care of Congress. Whenever brought into competition with the like industries of other countries, our fishermen, as well as our manufacturers of fishing appliances and preparers of fish products, have maintained a foremost place. I suggest that Congress create a commission to consider the general question of our rights in the fisheries and the means of opening to our citizens, under just and enduring conditions, the richly stocked fishing waters and sealing grounds of British North America . . .

At no time in our national history has there been more manifest need of close and lasting relations with a neighboring state than now exists with respect to Mexico. The rapid influx of our capital and enterprise into that country shows, by what has already been accomplished, the vast reciprocal advantages which must attend the progress of its internal development.

The treaty of commerce and navigation of 1848 has been terminated by the Mexican Government, and in the absence of conventional engagements the rights of our citizens in Mexico now depend upon the domestic statutes of that Republic. There have been instances of harsh enforcement of the laws against our vessels and citizens in Mexico and of denial of the diplomatic resort for their protection. The initial step toward a better understanding has been taken in the negotiation by the commission authorized by Congress of a treaty which is still before the Senate awaiting its approval.

The provisions for the reciprocal crossing of the frontier by the troops in pursuit of hostile Indians have been prolonged for another year. The operations of the forces of both Governments against these savages have been successful, and several of their most dangerous bands have been captured or dispersed by the skill and valor of United States and Mexican soldiers fighting in a common cause.

The convention for the resurvey of the boundary from the Rio Grande to the Pacific having been ratified and exchanged, the preliminary reconnoissance therein stipulated has been effected. It now rests with Congress to make provision for completing the survey and relocating the boundary monuments.

A convention was signed with Mexico on July 13, 1882, providing for the rehearing of the cases of Benjamin Weil and the Abra Silver Mining Company, in whose favor awards were made by the late American and Mexican Claims Commission. That convention still awaits the consent of the Senate. Meanwhile, because of those charges of fraudulent awards which have made a new commission necessary, the Executive has directed the suspension of payments of the distributive quota received from Mexico. . . .

From the report of the Secretary of War it will be seen that in only a single instance has there been any disturbance of the quiet condition of our Indian tribes. A raid from Mexico into Arizona was made in March last by a small party of Indians, which was pursued by General Crook into the mountain regions from which it had come. It is confidently hoped that serious outbreaks will not again occur and that the Indian tribes which have for so many years disturbed the West will hereafter remain in peaceable submission.

I again call your attention to the present condition of our extended seacoast, upon which are so many large cities whose wealth and importance to the country would in time of war invite attack from modern armored ships, against which our existing defensive works could give no adequate protection. Those works were built before the introduction of modern heavy rifled guns into maritime warfare, and if they are not put in an efficient condition we may easily be subjected to humiliation by a hostile power greatly inferior to ourselves. As germane to this subject, I call your attention to the importance of perfecting our submarine-torpedo defenses. The board authorized by the last Congress to report upon the method which should be adopted for the manufacture of heavy ordnance adapted to modern warfare. has visited the principal iron and steel works in this country and in Europe. It is hoped that its report will soon be made, and that Congress will thereupon be disposed to provide suitable facilities and plant for the manufacture of such guns as are now imperatively needed.

On several occasions during the past year officers of the Army have at the request of the State authorities visited their militia encampments for inspection of the troops. From the reports of these officers I am induced to believe that the encouragement of the State militia organizations by the National Government would be followed by very gratifying results, and would afford it in sudden emergencies the aid of a large body of volunteers educated in the performance of military duties.

The Secretary of the Navy reports that under the authority of the acts of August 5, 1882, and March 3, 1883, the work of strengthening our Navy by the construction of modern vessels has been auspiciously begun. Three cruisers are in process of construction—the *Chicago,* of 4,500 tons displacement, and the *Boston* and *Atlanta,* each of 2,500 tons. They are to be built of steel, with the tensile strength and ductility prescribed by law, and in the combination of speed, endurance, and armament are expected to compare favorably with the best unarmored war vessels of other nations. A fourth vessel, the *Dolphin,* is to be constructed of similar material, and is intended to serve as a fleet dispatch boat.

The double-turreted monitors *Puritan, Amphitrite,* and *Terror* have been launched on the Delaware River and a contract has been made for the supply of their machinery. A similar monitor, the *Monadnock,* has been launched in California.

The Naval Advisory Board and the Secretary recommend the completion of the monitors, the construction of four gunboats, and also of three additional steel vessels like the *Chicago, Boston,* and *Dolphin.*

As an important measure of national defense, the Secretary urges also the immediate creation of an interior coast line of waterways across the peninsula of Florida, along the coast from Florida to Hampton Roads, between the Chesapeake Bay and the Delaware River, and through Cape Cod.

I feel found to impress upon the attention of Congress the necessity of continued progress in the reconstruction of the Navy. The condition of the public Treasury, as I have already intimated, makes the present an auspicious time for putting this branch of the service in a state of efficiency.

It is no part of our policy to create and maintain a Navy able to cope with that of the other great power of the world.

We have no wish for foreign conquest, and the peace which we have long enjoyed is in no seeming danger of interruption.

But that our naval strength should be made adequate for the defense of our harbors, the protection of our commercial interests, and the main tenance of our national honor is a proposition from which no patriotic citizen can hold his assent. . .

The Utah Commission has submitted to the Secretary of the Interior its second annual report. As a result of its labors in supervising the recent election in that Territory, pursuant to the act of March 22, 1882, it appears that persons by that act disqualified to the number of about 12,000, were excluded from the polls. This fact, however, affords little cause for congratulation, and I fear that it is far from indicating any real and substantial progress toward the extripation of polygamy. All the members elect of the legislature are Mormons. There is grave reason to believe that they are in sympathy with the practices that this Government is seeking to suppress, and that its efforts in that regard will be more likely to encounter their opposition than to receive their encouragement and support. Even if this view should happily be erroneous, the law under which the commissioners have been acting should be made more effective by the incorporation of some such stringent amendments as they recommend, and as were included in bill No. 2238 on the Calendar of the Senate at its last session.

I am convinced, however, that polygamy has become so strongly intrenched in the Territory of Utah that it is profitless to attack it with any but the stoutest weapons which constitutional legislation can fashion. I favor, therefore, the repeal of the act upon which the existing government depends, the assumption by the National Legislature of the entire political control of the Territory, and the establishment of a commission with such powers and duties as shall be delegated to it by law. . .

The commissioners who were appointed under the act of January 16, 1883, entitled "An act to regulate and improve the civil service of the United States," entered promptly upon the discharge of their duties.

A series of rules, framed in accordance with the spirit of the statute, was approved and promulgated by the President.

In some particulars wherein they seemed defective those rules were subsequently amended. It will be preceived that they discountenance any political or religious tests for admission to those offices of the public service to which the statute relates.

The act is limited in its original application to the classified clerkships in the several Executive Departments at Washington (numbering about 5,600) and to similar positions in customs districts and post-offices where as many as fifty persons are employed. A classification of these positions analogous to that existing in the Washington offices was duly made before the law went into effect. Eleven customs districts and twenty-three post-offices were thus brought under the immediate operation of the statute.

The annual report of the Civil Service Commission which will soon be submitted to Congress will doubtless afford the means of a more definite judgment than I am now prepared to express as to the merits of the new system. I am persuaded that its effects have thus far proved beneficial. Its practical methods appear to be adequate for the ends proposed, and there has been no serious difficulty in carrying them into effect. Since the 16th of July last no person, so far as I am aware, has been appointed to the public service in the classified portions thereof at any of the Departments, or at any of the post-offices and customs districts above named, except those certified by the Commission to be the most competent on the basis of the examinations held in conformity to the rules.

At the time when the present Executive entered upon his office his death, removal, resignation, or inability to discharge his duties would have left the Government without a constitutional head.

It is possible, of course, that a similar contingency may again arise unless the wisdom of Congress shall provide against its recurrence.

The Senate at its last session, after full consideration, passed an act relating to this subject, which will now, I trust, commend itself to the approval of both Houses of Congress.

The clause of the Constitution upon which must depend any law regulating the Presidential succession presents also for solution other questions of paramount importance.

These questions relate to the proper interpretation of the phrase "inability to discharge the powers and duties of said office," our organic law providing that when the President shall suffer from such inability the Presidential office shall devolve upon the Vice-President, who must himself under like circumstances give place to such officer as Congress may by law appoint to act as President.

I need not here set forth the numerous and interesting inquiries which are suggested by these words of the Constitution. They were fully stated in my first communication to Congress and have since been the subject of frequent deliberations in that body.

It is greatly to be hoped that these momentous questions will find speedy solution, lest emergencies may arise when longer delay will be impossible and any determination, albeit the wisest, may furnish cause for anxiety and alarm. . .

ON THE ILLINOIS-MICHIGAN CANAL
January 8, 1884

Arthur announced to Congress his acceptance of the Illinois-Michigan Canal presented to the Federal government by the State of Illinois.*

To the Senate and House of Representatives:

I submit a communication from the governor of the State of Illinois, with a copy of an act of the general assembly of that State tendering to the United States the cession of the Illinois and Michigan Canal upon condition that it shall be enlarged and maintained as a national waterway for commercial purposes.

The proposed cession is an element of the subject which Congress had under consideration in directing by the act of August 2, 1882, a survey for a canal from a point on the Illinois River at or near the town of Hennepin by the most practicable route to the Mississippi River at or above the city of Rock Island, the canal to be not less than 70 feet wide at the water line and not less than 7 feet in depth of water, and with capacity for vessels of at least 280 tons burden; and also a survey of the Illinois and Michigan Canal and an estimate of the cost of enlarging it to the dimensions of the proposed canal between Hennepin and the Mississippi River.

The surveys ordered in the above act have been completed and the report upon them is included in the last annual report of the Secretary of War, and a copy is herewith submitted. It is estimated in the report that by the enlargement of the Illinois and Michigan Canal and the construction of the proposed canal by the shortest route between Hennepin and the Mississippi River a direct and convenient thoroughfare for vessels of 280 tons burden may be opened from the Mississippi River to Lake Michigan at a cost of $8,110,286.65, and that the annual charge for maintenance would be $138,600.

It appears from these papers that the estimate yield of corn, wheat, and oats for 1882 in the States of Illinois, Wisconsin, Iowa, Minnesota, Kansas, and Nebraska was more than 1,000,000,000 bushels. It is claimed that if the cheap water transportation route which is now continuous from the Atlantic Ocean to Chicago is extended to the Upper Mississippi by such a canal a great benefit in the reduction of freight charges would result to the people of the Upper Mississippi Valley, whose productions I have only partly noted, not only upon their own shipments, but upon the articles od commerce used by them, which are now taken from the Eastern States bu water only as far as Chicago.

As a matter of great interest, especially to the citizens of that part of the country, I commend the general subject to your consideration.

ON THE RECONSTRUCTION OF THE NAVY
March 26, 1884

Throughout his Administration, Arthur continually pleaded with Congress to improve, maintain and modernize the navy. This speech was one such plea.

To the Senate and House of Representatives:

In my annual message I impressed upon Congress the necessity of continued progress in the reconstruction of the Navy. The recommendations in this direction of the Secretary of the Navy and of the Naval Advisory Board were submitted by me unaccompanied by specific expressions of approval. I now deem it my duty to advise that appropriations be made at the present session toward designing and commencing the construction of at least three additional steel cruisers and the four gunboats thus recommended, the cost of which, including their armament, will not exceed $4,283,000, of which sum one-half should be appropriated for the next fiscal year.

The *Chicago, Boston, Atlanta,* and *Dolphin* have been designed and are being built with care and skill, and there is every reason to believe that they will prove creditable and serviceable modern cruisers. Technical questions concerning the details of these or of additional vessels can not wisely be settled except by experts, and the Naval Advisory Board, organized by direction of Congress under the act of August 5, 1882, and consisting of three line officers, a naval constructor, and a naval engineer, selected "with reference only to character, experience, knowledge, and skill," and a naval architect and a marine engineer from civil life "of established reputation and standing as experts in naval or marine construction," is an appropriate authority to decide finally all such questions. I am unwilling to see the gradual reconstruction of our naval cruisers, now happily begun in con formity with modern requirements, delayed one full year for any unsubstantial reason.

Whatever conditions Congress may see fit to impose in order to secure judicious designs and honest and economical construction will be acceptable to me, but to relinquish or postpone the policy already deliberately declared will be, in my judgment, an act of national imprudence.

Appropriations should also be made without delay for finishing the four double-turreted monitors, the *Puritan, Amphitrite, Terror,* and *Monadnock,* and for procuring their armament and that of the *Miantonomoh.* Their hulls are built, and their machinery is under contract and approaching completion, except that of the *Monadnock,* on the Pacific coast. This should also be built, and the armor and heavy guns of all should be procured at the earliest practicable moment.

The total amount appropriated up to this time for the four vessels is $3,546,941.41 A sum not exceeding $3,838,769.62, including $866,725 for four powerful rifled cannon and for the remainder of the ordnance outfit, will complete and equip them for service. Of the sum required, only two millions need be appropriated for the next fiscal year. It is not expected that one of the monitors will be a match for the heaviest broadside ironclads which certain other Governments have constructed at a cost of four or five millions each, but they will be armored vessels of an approved and useful type, presenting limited surfaces for the shot of an enemy, and possessed of such seagoing capacity and offensive power as fully to answer our immediate necessities. Their completion having been determined upon in the recent legislation of Congress, no time should be lost in accomplishing the necessary object. . .

ON THE NEW ORLEANS CENTENNIAL EXPOSITION
June 9, 1884

Arthur appointed a Special Board made up of representatives from each executive department to plan and develop a Federal government exhibit to be presented at the New Orleans World Fair.

To the Senate and House of Representatives:

I transmit herewith, for the consideration of Congress, a letter and its accompanying estimate, submitted by the board charged with preparing a departmental exhibit for the World's Industrial and Cotton Centennial Exposition to be held at New Orleans, beginning December 1, 1884. This board was appointed by Executive order of May 13, 1884, and is composed of representatives of the several Executive Departments, the Department of Agriculture, and the Smithsonian Institution. It is charged with the important and responsible duty of making arrangements for a complete and harmonious collection of the articles and materials deemed desirable to place on exhibition, in illustration of the resources of the country, its methods of governmental administration, and its means of offense and defense.

The board submits an estimate calling for an appropriation of $588,000 to accomplish the desired end. That amount is distributed among the Departments as shown in the table. The War, Navy and Interior Departments call for the largest share, representing as they do the national defenses by land and sea, the progress of naval architecture and ordnance, the geological survey and mineral wealth of the Territories, the treatment of the Indians, and the education of the masses, all of which admit of varied and instructive exhibits. The Smithsonian Institution, having under its general care the National Museum and the Fish Commission, is prepared to make a display second in interest to none of modern days. The remaining Departments can present instructive and interesting exhibits, which will attract popular attention and convey an idea of their extensively ramified duties and of the many points where they beneficially affect the life of the people as a nation and as individuals.

The exhibit of the Government at the Centennial Exhibition held at Philadelphia in 1876 was admitted to be one of the most attractive features of that great national undertaking and a valuable addition to it. From men of intelligence and scientific attainments, at home and abroad, it received the highest encomiums, showing the interest it awakened among those whose lives are given to the improvement of the social and material condition of the people.

The production of such a display now on a more extensive plan is rendered possible by the advancement of science and invention during the eight years that have passed since the Philadelphia exhibit was collected.

The importance, purposes, and benefits of the New Orleans Exhibition are continental in their scope. Standing at the threshold of the almost unopened markets of Spanish and Portuguese America, New Oreleans is a natural gateway to their trade, and the exhibition offers to the people of Mexico and Central and South America an adequate knowledge of our farming implements, mental manufactures, cotton and woolen goods, and the like necessities of existence, in respect to which those countries are either deficient or supplied to a limited extent. The breaking down of the barriers which still separate us from the Republics of America whose productions so entirely complement our own will aid greatly in removing the disparity of commerical intercourse under which less than 10 per cent of our exports to to American countries.

I trust that Congress will realize the urgency of this recommendation and make its appropriation immediately available, so that the board may lose no time in undertaking the extensive preparations necessary to spread Mexico and Central and South America an adequate knowledge of our farming implements, mental manufactures, cotton and woolen goods, and the like necessities of existence, in respect to which those countries are either deficient or supplied to a limited extent. The breaking down of the barriers which still separate us from the Republics of America whose productions so entirely complement our own will aid greatly in removing the disparity of commerical intercourse under which less than 10 per cent of our exports to to American countries.

I trust that Congress will realize the urgency of this recommendation and make its appropriation immediately available, so that the board may lose no time in undertaking the extensive preparations necessary to spread a more intimate knowledge of our Government institutions and national resources among the people of our country and of neighboring states in a way to command the respect due it in the family of nations.

A PROCLAMATION ON THE INDIAN TERRITORY
July 1, 1884

Throughout his Administration, Arthur tried to safeguard the rights of American Indians as specified in a number of treaties that had been negotiated with them.

A PROCLAMATION

Whereas it is alleged that certain persons have within the territory and jurisdiction of the United States begun and set on foot preparations for an organized and forcible possession of and settlement upon the lands of what is known as the Oklahoma lands, in the Indian Territory, which Territory is designated, recognized, and described by the treaties and laws of the United States and by the executive authorities as Indian country, and as such is subject to occupation by Indian tribes only; and

Whereas the laws of the United States provide for the removal of all persons residing or being fround in said Indian Territory without express permission of the Interior Department:

Now, therefore, for the purpose of properly protecting the interests of the Indian nations and tribes in said Territory, and that settlers may not be induced to go into a country, at great expense to themselves, where they can not be allowed to remain, I, Chester A. Arthur, President of the United States, do admonish and warn all such persons so intending or preparing to remove upon said lands or into said Territory against any attempt to so remove or settle upon any of the lands of said Territory; and I do further warn and notify any and all such persons who do so offend that they will be speedily and immediately removed therefrom by the proper officers of the Interior Department, and, if necessary, the aid and assistance of the military forces of the United States will be invoked to remove all such intruders from the said Indian Territory. . .

VETO OF AN ACT FOR THE RELIEF OF FITZ-JOHN PORTER
July 2, 1884

General Fitz-John Porter had been court-martialed during the Civil War. Congress passed a bill to reinstate him and place his name on the retired list with full pay. Arthur vetoed the bill.

To the House of Representatives:

After careful consideration of the bill entitled "An act for the relief of Fitz John Porter," I herewith return it with my objections to that House of Congress in which it originated. Its enacting clause is in terms following:

That the President be, and he is hereby, authorized to nominate and, by and with the advice and consent of the Senate, to appoint Fitz John Porter, late a major-general of the United States Volunteers and a brevet brigadier-general and colonel of the Army, to the position of colonel in the Army of the United States, of the same grade and rank held by him at the time of his dismissal from the Army by sentence of court-martial promulgated January 27, 1863. * * *

It is apparent that should this bill become a law it will create a new office which can be filled by the appointment of the particular individual whom it specifies, and can not be filled otherwise; or it may be said with perhaps greater precision of statement that it will create a new office upon condition that the particular person designated shall be chosen to fill it. Such an act, as it seems to me, is either unnecessary and ineffective or it involves an encroachment by the legislative branch of the Government upon the authority of the Executive. As the Congress has no power under the Constitution to nominate or appoint an officer and can not lawfully impose upon the President the duty of nominating or appointing to office any particular individual of its own selection, this bill, if it can fairly be construed as requiring the President to make the nomination and, by and with the advice and consent of the Senate, the appointment which it authorizes, is in manifest violation of the Constitution. If such be not its just interpretation, it must be regarded as a mere enactment of advice and counsel, which lacks in the very nature of things the force of positive law and can serve no useful purpose upon the statute books.

There are other causes that deter me from giving this bill the sanction of my approval. The judgment of the court-martial by which more than twenty years since General Fitz John Porter was tried and convicted was pronounced by a tribunal composed of nine general officers of distinguished character and ability. Its investigation of the charges of which it found the accused guilty was thorough and conscientious, and its findings and sentence were in due course of law approved by Abraham Lincoln, then

President of the United States. Its legal competency, its jurisdiction of the accused and of the subject of the accusation, and the substantial regularity of all of its proceedings are matters which have never been brought into question. Its judgment, therefore, is final and conclusive in its character.

The Supreme Court of the United States has recently declared that a court-martial such as this was is the organism provided by law and clothed with the duty of administering justice in this class of cases. Its judgements, when approved, rest on the same basis and are surrounded by the same considerations which give conclusiveness to the judgments of other legal tribunals, including as well the lowest as the highest. It follows, accordingly, that when a lawfully constituted court-martial has duly declared its findings and its sentence and the same have been duly approved neither the President nor the Congress has any power to set them aside. The existence of such power is not openly asserted, nor perhaps is it necessarily implied, in the provisions of the bill which is before me, but when its enacting clauses are read in the light of the recitations of its preamble it will be seen that it seeks in effect the practical annulment of the findings and the sentence of a competent court-martial . . .

I have already, in the exercise of the pardoning power with which the President is vested by the Constitution, remitted the continuing penalty which had made it impossible for Fitz John Porter to hold any office of trust or profit under the Government of the United States; but I am unwilling to give my sanction to any legislation which shall practically annul and set at naught the solemn and deliberate conclusions of the tribunal by which he was convicted and of the President by whom its findings were examined and approved.

A PROCLAMATION ON QUARANTINE REGULATIONS
July 19, 1884

With the hordes of immigrants flocking to American shores during these years, the spread of contagious diseases became a major concern of the Arthur Administration.

A PROCLAMATION.

While quarantine regulations are committed to the several States, the General Government has reposed certain powers in the President, to be used at his discretion in preventing a threatened epidemic.

Feeling it my duty, I hereby call upon all persons who under existing systems in the several States are intrusted with the execution of quarantine regulations to be diligent and on the alert in order to prevent the introduction of the pestilence which we all regret to learn has made its appearance in some of the countries of Europe between which and the ports of the United States intercourse is direct and frequent.

I further advise that the cities and towns of the United States, whether on the coast or on the lines of interior communication, by sound sanitary regulations and the promotion of cleanliness, be prepared to resist the power of the disease and to mitigate its severity.

And I further direct the consuls of the United States in the ports where the pestilence has made or may make its appearance to exercise vigilance in carrying out the instructions heretofore given and incommunicating to the Government of the United States any information of value relating to the progress or treatment of the disease. . .

Given under my hand and the seal of the United States, at the city of Washington, this 19th day of July, A.D. 1884, and of the Independence of the United States the one hundred and ninth.

CHESTER A. ARTHUR.

FOURTH ANNUAL MESSAGE
December 1, 1884

In this, his last annual message to Congress, Arthur reviewed what he believed were the major accomplishments of his Administration.

To the Congress of the United States:

Since the close of your last session the American people, in the exercise of their highest right of suffrage, have chosen their Chief Magistrate for the four years ensuing.

When it is remembered that at no period in the country's history has the long political contest which customarily precedes the day of the national election been waged with greater fervor and intensity, it is a subject of general congratulation that after the controversy at the polls is over, and while the slight preponderance by which the issue had been determined was as yet unascertained, the public peace suffered no disturbance, but the people everywhere patiently and quietly awaited the result.

Nothing could more strikingly illustrate the temper of the American citizen, his love of order, and his loyalty to law. Nothing could more signally demonstrate the strength and wisdom of our political institutions.

Eight years have passed since a controversy concerning the result of a national election sharply called the attention of the Congress to the necessity of providing more precise and definite regulations for counting the electoral vote.

It is of the gravest importance that this question be solved before conflicting claims to the Presidency shall again distract the country, and I am persuaded that by the people at large any of the measures of relief thus far proposed would be preferred to continued inaction.

Our relations with all foreign powers continue to be amicable.

With Belgium a convention has been signed whereby the scope of present treaties has been so enlarged as to secure to citizens of either country within the jurisdiction of the other equal rights and privileges in the acquisition and alienation of property. A trade-marks treaty has also been concluded.

The war between Chile and Peru is at an end. For the arbitration of the claims of American citizens who during its continuance suffered through the acts of the Chilian authorities a convention will soon be negotiated.

The state of hostilities between France and China continues to be an embarrassing feature of our Eastern relations. The Chinese Government has promptly adjusted and paid the claims of American citizens whose property was destroyed in the recent riots in Canton. I renew the recommendation of my last annual message, that the Canton indemnity fund be returned to China.

The true interpretation of the recent treaty with that country permitting the restriction of Chinese immigration is likely to be again the subject of your deliberations. It may be seriously questioned whether the statute passed at the last session does not violate the treaty rights of certain Chinese who left this country with return certificates valid under the old law, and who now seem to be barred from relanding for lack of the certificates required by the new.

The recent purchase by citizens of the United States of a large trading fleet heretofore under the Chinese flag has considerably enhanced our commerical importance in the East. In view of the large number of vessels built or purchased by American citizens in other countries and exclusively employed in legitimate traffic between foreign ports under the recognized protection of our flag, it might be well to provide a uniform rule for their registration and documentation, so that the *bona fide* property rights of our citizens therein shall be duly evidenced and properly guarded.

Pursuant to the advice of the Senate at the last session, I recognized the flag of the International Association of the Kongo as that of a friendly government, avoiding in so doing any prejudgment of conflicting territorial claims in that region. Subsequently, in execution of the expressed wish of the Congress, I appointed a commercial agent for the Kongo basin.

The importance of the rich prospective trade of the Kongo Valley has led to the general conviction that it should be open to all nations upon equal terms. At an international conference for the consideration of this subject called by the Emperor of Germany, and now in session at Berlin, delegates are in attendance on behalf of the United States. Of the results of the conference you will be duly advised.

The Government of Korea has generously aided the efforts of the United States minister to secure suitable premises for the use of the legation. As the conditions of diplomatic intercourse with Eastern nations demand that the legation premises be owned by the represented power, I advise that an appropriation be made for the acquisition of this property by the Government. The United States already possess valuable premises at Tangier as a gift from the Sultan of Morocco. As is stated hereafter, they have lately received a similar gift from the Siamese Government. The Government of Japan stands ready to present to us extensive grounds at Tokyo whereon to erect a suitable building for legation, court-house, and jail, and similar privileges can probably be secured in China and Persia. The owning of such premises would not only effect a large saving of the present rentals, but would permit of the due assertion of extraterritorial rights in those countries, and would the better serve to maintain the dignity of the United States.

The failure of Congress to make appropriation for our representation at the autonomous court of the Khedive has proved a serious embarrassment in our intercourse with Egypt; and in view of the necessary intimacy of diplomatic relationship due to the participation of this Government as one of the treaty powers in all matters of administration there affecting the rights of foreigners, I advise the restoration of the agency and consulate-general at Cairo on its former basis. I do not conceive it to be the wish of Congress that the United States should withdraw altogether from the honorable position they have hitherto held with respect to the Khedive, or that citizens of this Republic residing or sojourning in Egypt should here-after be without the aid and protection of a competent representative.

With France the traditional cordial relationship continues. The colossal statue of Liberty Enlightening the World, the generous gift of the people of France, is expected to reach New York in May next. I suggest that Con-gressional action be taken in recognition of the spirit which has prompted this gift and in aid of the timely completion of the pedestal upon which it is to be placed.

Our relations with Germany, a country which contributes to our own some of the best elements of citizenship, continue to be cordial. The United States have extradition treaties with several of the German States, but by reason of the confederation of those States under the imperial rule the application of such treaties is not as uniform and comprehensive as the interests of the two countries require. I propose, therefore, to open negotia-tions for a single convention of extradition to embrace all the territory of the Empire.

It affords me pleasure to say that our intercourse with Great Britain continues to be of a most friendly character.

The Government of Hawaii has indicated its willingness to continue for seven years the provisions of the existing reciprocity treaty. Such continu-ance, in view of the relations of that country to the American system of States, should, in my judgment, be favored.

The revolution in Hayti against the established Government has ter-minated. While it was in progress it became necessary to enforce our neutrality laws by instituting proceedings against individuals and vessels charged with their infringement. These prosecutions were in all cases successful.

Much anxiety has lately been displayed by various European Govern-ments, and especially by the Government of Italy, for the abolition of our import duties upon works of art. It is well to consider whether the present discrimination in favor of the productions of American artists abroad is not likely to result, as they themselves seem very generally to believe it may, in the practical exclusion of our painters and sculptors from the rich fields for observation, study, and labor which they have hitherto enjoyed.

There is prospect that the long-pending revision of the foreign treaties of Japan may be concluded at a new conference to be held at Tokyo. While this Government fully recognizes the equal and independent station of

Japan in the community of nations, it would not oppose the general adoption of such terms of compromise as Japan may be disposed to offer in furtherance of a uniform policy of intercourse with Western nations.

During the past year the increasing good will between our own Government and that of Mexico has been variously manifested. The treaty of commercial reciprocity concluded January 20, 1883, has been ratified and awaits the necessary tariff legislation of Congress to become effective. This legislation will, I doubt not, be among the first measures to claim your attention.

A full treaty of commerce, navigation, and consular rights is much to be desired, and such a treaty I have reason to believe that the Mexican Government stands ready to conclude.

Some embarrassment has been occasioned by the failure of Congress at its last session to provide means for the due execution of the treaty of July 29, 1882, for the resurvey of the Mexican boundary and the relocation of boundary monuments.

With the Republic of Nicaragua a treaty has been concluded which authorizes the construction by the United States of a canal, railway, and telegraph line across the Nicaraguan territory.

By the terms of this treaty 60 miles of the river San Juan, as well as Lake Nicaragua, an inland sea 40 miles in width, are to constitute a part of the projected enterprise.

·This leaves for actual canal construction 17 miles on the Pacific side and 36 miles on the Atlantic. To the United States, whose rich territory on the Pacific is for the ordinary purposes of commerce practically cut off from communication by water with the Atlantic ports, the political and commercial advantages of such a project can scarcely be overestimated.

It is believed that when the treaty is laid before you the justice and liberality of its provisions will command universal approval at home and abroad. . .

The final disposition of pending questions with Venezuela has not as yet been reached, but I have good reason to expect an early settlement which will provide the means of reexamining the Caracas awards in conformity with the expressed desire of Congress, and which will recognize the justice of certain claims preferred against Venezuela.

The Central and South American Commission appointed by authority of the act of July 7, 1884, will soon proceed to Mexico. It has been furnished with instructions which will be laid before you. They contain a statement of the general policy of the Government for enlarging its commerical intercourse with American States. The commissioners have been actively preparing for their responsible task by holding conferences in the principal cities with merchants and others interested in Central and South American trade.

The International Meridian Conference lately convened in Washington upon the invitation of the Government of the United States was composed of representatives from twenty-five nations. The conference concluded its labors on the 1st of November, having with substantial unanimity agreed upon the meridian of Greenwich as the starting point whence longitude is to be computed through 180 degrees eastward and westward, and upon the adoption, for all purposes for which it may be found convenient of a universal day which shall begin at midnight on the initial meridian and whose hours shall be counted from zero up to twenty-four.

The formal report of the transactions of this conference will be hereafter transmitted to the Congress. . .

Our existing naturalization laws also need revision. Those sections relating to persons residing without the limits of the United States in 1795 and 1798 have now only a historical interest. Section 2172, recognizing the citizenship of the children of naturalized parents, is ambiguous in its terms and partly obsolete. There are special provisions of law favoring the naturalization of those who serve in the Army or in merchant vessels, while no similar privileges are granted those who serve in the Navy or the Marine Corps.

"An uniform rule of naturalization" such as the Constitution contemplates should, among other things, clearly define the status of persons born within the United States subject to a foreign power (section 1992) and of minor children of fathers who have declared their intention to become citizens but have failed to perfect their naturalization. It might be wise to provide for a central bureau of registry, wherein should be filed authenticated transcripts of every record of naturalization in the several Federal and State courts, and to make provision also for the vacation or cancellation of such record in cases where fraud had been practiced upon the court by the applicant himself or where he had renounced or forfeited his acquired citizenship. A just and uniform law in this respect would strengthen the hands of the Government in protecting its citizens abroad and would pave the way for the conclusion of treaties of naturalization with foreign countries. . . .

The Secretary of War submits the report of the Chief of Engineers as to the practicability of protecting our important cities on the seaboard by fortifications and other defenses able to repel modern methods of attack. The time has now come when such defenses can be prepared with confidence that they will not prove abortive, and when the possible result of delay in making such preparation is seriously considered delay seems inexcusable. For the most important cities—those whose destruction or capture would be a national humiliation—adequate defenses, inclusive of guns, may be made by the gradual expenditure of $60,000,000—a sum much less than a victorious enemy could levy as a contribution. An appropriation of about one-tenth of that amount is asked to begin the work, and I concur with the Secretary of War in urging that it be granted.

The War Department is proceeding with the conversion of 10-inch smoothbore guns into 8-inch rifles by lining the former with tubes of forged steel or of coil wrought iron. Fifty guns will be thus converted within the year. This, however, does not obviate the necessity of providing means for the construction of guns of the highest power both for the purposes of coast defense and for the armament of war vessels.

The report of the Gun Foundry Board, appointed April 2, 1883, in pursuance of the act of March 3, 1883, was transmitted to Congress in a special message of February 18, 1884. In my message of March 26, 1884, I called attention to the recommendation of the board that the Government should encourage the production at private steel works of the required material for heavy cannon, and that two Governement factories, one for the Army and one for the Navy, should be established for the fabrication of guns from such material. No action having been taken the board was subsequently reconvened to determine more fully the plans and estimates necessary for carrying out its recommendation. It has received information which indicates that there are responsible steel manufacturers in this country who, although not provided at present with the necessary plant, are willing to construct the same and to make bids for contracts with the Government for the supply of the requisite material for the heaviest guns adapted to modern warfare if a guaranteed order of sufficient magnitude, accompanied by a positive appropriation extending over a series of years, shall be made by Congress. All doubts as to the feasibility of the plan being thus removed, I renew my recommendation that such action be taken by Congress as will enable the Government to construct its own ordnance upon its own territory, and so to provide the armaments demanded by considerations of national safety and honor.

The report of the Secretary of the Navy exhibits the progress whichhas been made on the new steel cruisers authorized by the acts of August 5, 1882, and March 3, 1883. Of the four vessels under contract, one , the *Chicago,* of 4,500 tons, is more than half finished; the *Atlanta,* of 3,000 tons, has been successfully launched, and her machinery is now fitting; the *Boston,* also of 3,000 tons, is ready for launching, and the *Dolphin,* a dispatch steamer of 1,500 tons, is ready for delivery.

Certain adverse criticisms upon the designs of these cruisers are discussed by the Secretary, who insists that the correctness of the conclusions reached by the Advisory Board and by the Department has been demonstrated by recent developments in shipbuilding abroad.

The machinery of the double-turreted monitors *Puritan, Terror,* and *Amphitrite,* contracted for under the act of March 3, 1883, is in progress of construction. No work has been done during the past year on their armor for lack of the necessary appropriations. A fourth monitor, the *Monadnock,* still remains unfinished at the navy-yard in California. It is recommended that early steps be taken to complete these vessels and to provide also an armament for the monitor *Miantonomoh.*

The recommendations of the Naval Advisory Board, approved by the Department, comprise the construction of one steel crusier of 4,500 tons, one cruiser of 3,000 tons, two heavily armed gunboats, one light cruising gunboat, one dispatch vessel armed with Hochkiss cannon, one armored ram, and three torpedo boats. The general designs, all of which are calculated to meet the existing wants of the service, are now well advanced, and the construction of the vessels can be undertaken as soon as you shall grant the necessary authority. . .

In this the last of the stated messages that I shall have the honor to transmit to the Congress of the United States I can not too strongly urge upon its attention the duty of restoring our Navy as rapidly as possible to the high state of efficiency which formerly characterized it. As the long peace that has lulled us into a sense of fancied security may at any time be disturbed, it is plain that the policy of strengthening this arm of the service is dictated by considerations of wise economy, of just regard for our future tranquillity, and of true appreciation of the dignity and honor of the Republic. . . .

In the course of this communication reference has more than once been made to the policy of this Government as regards the extension of our foreign trade. It seems proper to declare the general principles that should in my opinion, underlie our national efforts in this direction.

The main conditions of the problem may be thus stated:

We are a people apt in mechanical pursuits and fertile in invention. We cover a vast extent of territory rich in agricultural products and in nearly all the raw materials necessary for successful manufacture. We have a system of productive establishments more than sufficient to supply our own demands. The wages of labor are nowhere else so great. The scale of living of our artisan classes is such as tends to secure their personal comfort and the development of those higher moral and intellectual qualities that go to the making of good citizens. Our system of tax and tariff legislation is yielding a revenue which is in excess of the present needs of the Government.

These are the elements from which it is sought to devise a scheme by which, without unfavorably changing the condition of the workingman, our merchant marine shall be raised from its enfeebled condition and new markets provided for the sale beyond our borders of the manifold fruits of our industrial enterprises.

The problem is complex and can be solved by no single measure of innovation or reform.

The countries of the American continent and the adjacent islands are for the United States the natural marts of supply and demand. It is from them that we should obtain what we do not produce or do not produce in sufficiency, and it is to them that the surplus productions of our fields, our mills, and our workshops should flow, under conditions that will equalize or favor them in comparison with foreign competition. . .

On the 29th of February last I transmitted to the Congress the first annual report of the Civil Service Commission, together with communications from the heads of the several Executive Departments of the Government respecting the practical workings of the law under which the Commission had been acting. The good results therein foreshadowed have been more than realized.

The system has fully answered the expectations of its friends in securing competent and faithful public servants and in protecting the appointing officers of the Government from the pressure of personal importunity and from the labor of examining the claims and pretensions of rival candidates for public employment.

The law has had the unqualified support of the President and of the heads of the several Departments, and the members of the Commission have performed their duties with zeal and fidelity. Their report will shortly be submitted, and will be accompanied by such recommendations for enlarging the scope of the existing statute as shall commend themselves to the Executive and the Commissioners charged with its administration. . .

Certain of the measures that seem to me necessary and expedient I have now, in obedience to the Constitution, recommended for your adoption.

As respects others of no less importance I shall content myself with renewing the recommendations already made to the Congress, without restating the grounds upon which such recommendations were based.

The preservation of forests on the public domain, the granting of Government aid for popular education, the amendment of the Federal Constitution so as to make effective the disapproval by the President of particular items in appropriation bills, the enactment of statutes in regard to the filling of vacancies in the Presidential office, and the determining of vexed questions respecting Presidential inability are measures which may justly receive your serious consideration.

As the time draws nigh when I am to retire from the public service, I can not refrain from expressing to the members of the National Legislature with whom I have been brought into personal and official intercourse my sincere appreciation of their unfailing courtesy and of their harmonious cooperation with the Executive in so many measures calculated to promote the best interests of the nation.

And to my fellow-citizens generally I acknowledge a deep sense of obligation for the support which they have accorded me in my administration of the executive department of this Government.

ON THE NICARAGUAN INTEROCEANIC CANAL TREATY
December 10, 1884

Although Arthur requested ratification of this treaty, the Senate refused to act during the remainder of his Administration. Cleveland, as President, did not present the treaty for ratification, and it was never approved.

To the Senate of the United States:

I transmit hereiwth to the Senate, for consideration with a view to ratification, a treaty signed on the 1st of December with the Republic of Nicaragua, providing for the construction of an interoceanic canal across the territory of that State.

The negotiation of this treaty was entered upon under a conviction that it was imperatively demanded by the present and future political and material interests of the United States.

The establishment of water communication between the Atlantic and Pacific coasts of the Union is a necessity, the accomplishment of which, however, within the territory of the United States is a physical impossibility. While the enterprise of our citizens has responded to the duty of creating means of speedy transit by rail between the two oceans, these great achievements are inadequate to supply a most important requisite of national union and prosperity.

For all maritime purposes the States upon the Pacific are more distant from those upon the Atlantic than if separated by either ocean alone. Europe and Africa are nearer to New York, and Asia nearer to California, than are these two great States to each other by sea. Weeks of steam voyage or months under sail are consumed in the passage around the Horn, with the disadvantage of traversing tempertuous waters or risking the navigation of the Straits of Magellan.

A nation like ours can not rest satisfied with such a separation of its mutually dependent members. We possess an ocean border of considerably over 10,000 miles on the Atlantic and Gulf of Mexico, and, including Alaska, of some 10,000 miles on the Pacific. Within a generation the western coast has developed into an empire, with a large and rapidly growing population, with vast, but partially developed, resources. At the present rate of increase the end of the century will see us a commonwealth of perhaps nearly 100,000,000 inhabitants, of which the West should have a considerably larger and richer proportion than now. Forming one nation in interests and aims, the East and the West are more widely disjoined for all purposes of direct and economical intercourse by water and of national defense against maritime aggression than are most of the colonies of other powers from their mother country.

The problem of establishing such water communication has long attracted attention. Many projects have been formed and surveys have been made of all possible available routes. As a knowledge of the true topical conditions of the Isthmus was gained, insurperable difficulties in one case and another became evident, until by a process of elimination only two routes remained within range of profitable achievement, one by way of Panama and the other across Nicaragua.

The treaty now laid before you provides for such a waterway through the friendly territory of Nicaragua.

I invite your special attention to the provisions of the convention itself as best evidencing its scope.

From respect to the independent sovereignty of the Republic, through those cooperation the project can alone be realized, the stipulations of the treaty look to the fullest recognition and protection of Nicaraguan rights in the premises. The United States have no motive or desire for territorial acquisition or political control beyond the present borders, and none such is contemplated by this treaty. The two Governments unite in framing this scheme as the sole means by which the work, as indislensable to the one as to the other, can be accomplished under such circumstances as to prevent alike the possibility of conflict between them and of interference from without.

The canal is primarily a domestic means of water communication between the Atlantic and Pacific shores of the two countries which unite for its construction, the one contributing the territory and the other furnishing the money therefor. Recognizing the advantages which the world's commerce must derive from the work, appreciating the benefit of enlarged use to the canal itself by contributing to its maintenance and by yielding an interest return on the capital invested therein, and inspired by the belief that any grat enterprise which inures to the general benefit of the world is in some sort a trust for the common advancement of mankind, the two Governments have by this treaty provided for its peaceable use by all nations on equal terms, while reserving to the coasting trade of both countries (in which none but the contracting parties are interested) the privilege of favoring tolls.

The treaty provides for the construction of a railway and telegraph line, if deemed advisable, as accessories to the canal, as both may be necessary for the economical construction of the work and probably in its operation when completed.

The terms of the treaty as to the protection of the canal, while scrupulously confirming the sovereignty of Nicaragua, amply secure that State and the work itself from the possible contingencies of the future which it may not be within the sole power of Nicaragua to meet.

From a purely commercial point of view the completion of such a waterway opens a most favorable prospect for the future of our country. . .

The political effect of the canal will be to knit closer the States now depending upon railway corporations for all commercial and personal intercourse, and it will not only cheapen the cost of transportation, but will free individuals from the possibility of unjust discriminations.

It will bring the European grain markets of demand within easy distance of our Pacific States, and will give to the manufacturers on the Atlantic seaboard economical access to the cities of China, thus breaking down the barrier which separates the principal manufacturing centers of the United States from the markets of the vast population of Asia, and placing the Eastern States of the Union for all purposes of trade midway between Europe and Asia. In point of time the gain for sailing vessels would be great, amounting from New York to San Francisco to a saving of seventy-five days; to Hongkong, of twenty-seven days; to Shanghai, of thirty-four days, and to Callao, of fifty-two days. . .

The purely pecuniary prospects of the canal as an investment are subordinate to the great national benefits to accrue from it; but it seems evident that the work, great as its cost may appear, will be a measure of prudent economy and foresight if undertaken simply to afford our own vessels a free waterway, for its far-reaching results will, even within a few years in the life of a nation, amply repay the expenditure by the increase of national prosperity. Further, the canal would unquestionably be immediately remunerative. It offers a shorter sea voyage, with more continuously favoring winds, between the Atlantic ports of America and Europe and the countries of the East than any other practicable route, and with lower tolls, by reason of its lesser cost, the Nicaraguan route must be the interoceanic highway for the bulk of the world's trade between the Atlantic and the Pacific.

So strong is this consideration that it offers an abundant guaranty for the investment to be made, as well as for the speedy payment of the loan of four millions which the treaty stipulates shall be made to Nicaragua for the construction of internal improvements to serve as aids to the business of the canal.

I might suggest many other considerations in detail, but it seems unnecessary to do so. Enough has been said to more than justify the practical utility of the measure. I therefore commit it to the Congress in the confident expectation that it will receive approval, and that by appropriate legislation means may be provided for inaugurating the work without delay after the treaty shall have been ratified. . .

ON COMMERCIAL RECIPROCITY WITH SPAIN
December 10, 1884

*In foreign policy, Arthur was an innovator. Commercial recipro-
city was one of the primary desires of the Administration. However, Congress refused to ratify this treaty, as well as a number
of others.*

To the Senate of the United States:

I transmit herewith, for consideration by the Senate with a view to
advising and consenting to its ratification, a convention for commercial
reciprocity between the United States and Spain, providing for an intimate and favored exchange of products with the islands of Cuba and
Puerto Rico, which convention was signed at Madrid on the 18th
ultimo.

The negotiations for this convention have been in progress since April
last, in pursuance of the understanding reached by the two Governments
on the 2d of January, 1884, for the improvement of commercial relations
between the United States and the Spanish Antilles, by the eighth article
of which both Governments engaged "to begin at once negotiations for
a complete treaty of commerce and navigation between the United States
of America and the said Provinces of Cuba and Puerto Rico." Although
this clause was by common consent omitted from the substitutionary
agreement of February 13, 1884 (now in force until replaced by this convention being carried into effect), the obligation to enter upon such a
negotiation was deemed to continue. With the best desire manifest on both
sides to reach a common accord, the negotiation has been necessarily
protracted, owing to the complexity of the details to be incorporated in
order that the convention might respond to the national policy of intercourse with the neighboring communities of the American system, which
is outlined in my late annual message to the Congress in the following words:

> The conditions of these treaties should be the free admission of
> such merchandise as this country does not produce, in return for
> the admission free or under a favored scheme of duties of our own
> products, the benefits of such exchange to apply only to goods
> carried under the flag of the parties to the contract; the removal
> on both sides from the vessels so privileged of all tonnage dues and
> national imposts, so that those vessels may ply unhindered between
> our ports and those of the other contracting parties, though
> without infringing on the reserved home coasting trade; the re-
> moval or reduction of burdens on the exported products of those
> countries coming within the benefits of the treaties, and the

avoidance of the technical restrictions and penalties by which our intercourse with those countries is at present hampered.

A perusal of the convention now submitted will suffice to show how fully it carried out the policy of intercourse thus announced. I commend it to you in the confident expectation that it will receive your sanction.

It does not seem necessary to my present purpose to enter into detailed consideration of the many immediate and prospective advantages which will flow from this convention to our productions and our shipping interests.

ON THE CREEK AND SEMINOLE LANDS
January 27, 1885

Arthur ordered all trespassers on Indian lands to be removed; by force if necessary. He then reported the situation to Congress.

To the Senate of the United States:

In response to the resolution of the Senate of the 22nd instant, setting forth that—

Whereas the United States, in 1866, acquired from the Creek and Seminole Indians by treaty certain lands situated in the Territory, a portion of which have remained unoccupied until the present time; and

Whereas a widely extended belief exists that such unoccupied lands are public lands of the United States, and as such subject to homestead and preemption settlement, and pursuant to such belief a large number of citizens of the United States have gone upon them claiming the right to settle and acquire title thereto under the general land laws of the United States; and

Whereas it is understood that the President of the United States does not regard said lands as open to settlement and believes it to be his duty to remove all persons who go upon the same claiming the right to settle thereon, and for that purpose has directed the expulsion of the persons now on said lands by the use of military force, and there seems to be a probability of a conflict growing out of the attempt to expel said persons so claiming right and attempting to settle: Therefore

Resolved, That the President be requested to advise the Senate as to the status of the lands in question as viewed by the Executive, the action taken, if any, to expel persons seeking to settle thereon, and the reasons for the same, together with any other information in his possession bearing upon the existing controversy—

I have the honor to state that the matter was referred to the Secretaries of War and the Interior and to transmit herewith their respective reports thereon, dated the 26th instant.

The report of the Commissioner of Indian Affairs accompanying that of the Secretary of the Interior recites fully the provisions of the treaties made with the Indian tribes ceding the lands in question to the United States, showing the condition and purposes expressed in said treaties regarding said lands, as well as the action taken with reference thereto, from which it will be seen that they are not open to settlement under any laws of the United States.

The report of the Secretary of War shows the action of the military authorities at the request of the Interior Department under section 2147 of the Revised Statutes.

The status of these lands was considered by my predecessor, President Hayes, who on the 26th day of April, 1879, issued a proclamation warning all persons intending to go upon said lands withhout proper permission of the Interior Department that they would be speedily and immediately removed therefrom according to the laws made and provided, and that if necessary the aid and assistance of the military forces of the United States would be invoked to carry into proper execution the laws of the United States referring thereto. A similar proclamation was issued by President Hayes on the 12th day of February, 1880. On the 1st day of July, 1884, I considered it to be my duty to issue a proclamation of like import.

These several proclamations were at the request of the Secretary of the Interior.

As will be seen by the report of the Secretary of War, the military forces of the United States have been repeatedly employed to remove intruders from the lands in question, and that notwithstanding such removals and in disregard of law and the Executive proclamations a large body of intruders is now within the territory in question, and that an adequate force of troops has been ordered to remove the intruders and is now being concentrated for that purpose.

None of the land or general laws of the United States have been extended over these lands except as to the punishment for crimes and other provisions contained in the intercourse act which relate to trade and the introduction of spirituous liquors and arms among Indians, and do not sanction settlement. It is clear that no authorized settlement can be made by any person in the territory in question.

Until the existing status of these lands shall have been changed by agreement with the Indians interested, or in some other manner as may be determined by Congress, the treaties heretofore made with the Indians should be maintained and the power of the Government to the extent necessary should be exercised to keep off intruders and all unauthorized persons.

A PROCLAMATION ON CANADIAN RECIPROCITY
January 31, 1885

An amicable treaty was negotiated with Canada concerning tonnage duties. Arthur proclaimed it in effect on this day.

A PROCLAMATION

Whereas satisfactory evidence has been received by me that upon vessels of the United States arriving in ports of the Province of Ontario, in the Dominion of Canada, or arriving at any port in the island of Monserrat, in the West Indies, or at Panama or Aspinwall, United States of Colombia, or at the ports of San Juan and Mayaguez, in the island of Puerto Rico, no duty is imposed by the ton as tonnage tax or as light money, and that no other equivalent tax on vessels of the United States is imposed at said ports by the governments to which said ports are immediately subject; and

Whereas by the provisions of section 14 of an act approved June 26, 1884, "to remove certain burdens on the American merchant marine and encourage the American foreign carrying trade, and for other purposes," the President of the United States is authorized to suspend the collection in ports of the United States from vessels arriving from any ports in the Dominion of Canada, Newfoundland, the Bahama Islands, the Bermuda Islands, the West India Islands, Mexico, and Central America down to and including Aspinwall and Panama of so much of the duty at the rate of 3 cents per ton as may be in excess of the tonnage and light-house dues, or other equivalent tax or taxes, imposed on American vessels by the government of the foreign country in which such port is situated:

Now, therefore, I, Chester A. Arthur, President of the United States of America, by virtue of the authority vested in me by the act and section hereinbefore mentioned, do hereby declare and proclaim that on and after the first Tuesday in February, 1885, the collection of said tonnage duty of 3 cents per ton shall be suspended as regards all vessels arriving in any port of the United States from any port in the Province of Ontario, in the Dominion of Canada, or from a port in the island of Monserrat, in the West Indies, or from the ports of Panama and Aspinwall, or the ports of San Juan and Mayaguez, in the island of Puerto Rico.

ON GENERAL ULYSSES S. GRANT
February 3, 1885

Arthur gratefully accepted, for the government, momentoes and testimonials belonging to General Grant. The collection was given to the United States by the General's wife, Julia Dent Grant.

To the Senate and House of Representatives:

I take especial pleasure in laying before Congress the generous offer made by Mrs. Grant to give to the Government, in perpetual trust, the swords and military (and civil) testimonials lately belonging to General Grant. A copy of the deed of trust and of a letter addressed to me by Mr. William H. Vanderbilt, which I transmit herewith, will explain the nature and motives of this offer.

Appreciation of General Grant's achievements and recognition of his just fame have in part taken the shape of numerous mementoes and gifts which, while dear to him, possess for the nation an exception interest. These relics, of great historical value, have passed into the hands of another, whose considerate action has restored the collection to Mrs. Grant as a life trust, on the condition that at the death of General Grant or sooner, at Mrs. Grant's option, it should become the property of the Government, as set forth in the accompanying papers. In the exercise of the option thus given her Mrs. Grant elects that the trust shall forthwith determine, and asks that the Government designate a suitable place of deposit and a responsible custodian for the collection.

The nature of this gift and the value of the relics which the generosity of a private citizen, joined to the high sense of public regard which animates Mrs. Grant, have thus placed at the disposal of the Government, demand full and signal recognition on behalf of the nation at the hands of its representatives. I therefore ask Congress to take suitable action to accept the trust and to provide for tis secure custody, at the same time recording the appreciative gratitude of the people of the United States to the donors.

In this connection I may pertinently advert to the pending legislation of the Senate and House of Representatives looking to a national recognition of General Grant's eminent services by providing the means for his restoration to the Army on the retired list. That Congress, by taking such action, will give expression to the almost universal desire of the people of this nation is evident, and I earnestly urge the passage of an act similar to Senate bill No. 2530, which, while not interfering with the constitutional prerogative of appointment, will enable the President in his discretion to nominate General Grant as general upon the retired list.

A PROCLAMATION ON NICARAGUAN RECIPROCITY
February 26, 1885

This reciprocity treaty was one of the very few approved by the Senate. Arthur proclaimed it in operation in this message.

A PROCLAMATION

Whereas satisfactory evidence has been received by me that upon vessels of the United States arriving at the port of San Juan del Norte (Greytown), Nicaragua, no duty is imposed by the ton as tonnage tax or as light money, and that no other equivalent tax on vessels of the United States is imposed at said port by the Government of Nicaragua; and

Whereas, by the provisions of section 14 of an act approved June 26, 1884 "to remove certain burdens on the American merchant marine and encourage the American foreign carrying trade, and for other purposes," the President of the United States is authorized to suspend the collection in ports of the United States from vessels arriving from any port in the Dominion of Canada, Newfoundland, the Bahama Islands, the Bermuda Islands, the West India Islands, Mexico, and Central America down to and including Aspinwall and Panama of so much of the duty at the rate of 3 cents per ton as may be in excess of the tonnage and light-house dues, or other equivalent tax or taxes, imposed on American vessels by the government of the foreign country in which such port is situated:

Now, therefore, I, Chester A. Arthur, President of the United States of America, by virtue of the authority vested in me by the act and section hereinbefore mentioned, do hereby declare and proclaim that on and after the first Tuesday in March, 1885, the collection of said tonnage duty of 3 cents per ton shall be suspended as regards all vessels arriving in any port of the United States from the port of San Juan del Norte (Greytown), Nicaragua.

BIBLIOGRAPHICAL AIDS

Because of the nature of the Garfield-Arthur Administration, this must be a combined bibliography. There is a rather large collection of Garfield's papers at the Library of Congress. These include: Manuscript Journal, 1872-1881; Letters sent, 1868-1881; Letters received 1852-1881; Public utterances, 1852-1881; and Notes and Miscellaneous papers, 1859-1881. In addition, the New York Public Library houses a small collection of Garfield papers dealing entirely with details of Garfield's last illness. Both of these collections are available on microfilm, and an index has been prepared for them. Only a few biographies of Garfield have been done, the latest written in 1931. As far as Arthur is concerned, no voluminous stock of papers have been left to posterity. The Library of Congress holds some sixty-five letters addressed to him during his Presidency. His brother's papers contain a few letters written by him several years before. There are some unpublished archives in Washington which are fruitful in somewhat lesser degree. Whatever published materials are available have been microfilmed and indexed. Only one biography of Arthur has been written as of this date. As a result, any biographer of Arthur must rely upon the papers of political associates and opponents for most of his information.

SOURCE MATERIALS

Arthur, Chester A., in *Messages and Papers of the Presidents, 1789-1897,* James D. Richardson, ed., 10 vols. Washington, 1896-1899, VIII, 33-294.

Chase Papers (Library of Congress). Indexed and microfilmed.

Congressional Globe, 1863-1873.

Congressional Record, 1873-1881, 1881-1885.

Credit Mobilier Report. House Reports, No. 77, 42nd Cong., 3rd Session, pp. 5, 6, 20, 28, 40, 91, 92, 128-131, 136, 180, 181, 223, 228, 303, 353, 361, 450-451, 471.

Documents Issued by the Union Republican Congressional Committee, 1880. 2 vols. Washington, 1880.

Garfield, James A. "A Century of Congress." *Atlantic Monthly.* July 1877.

Garfield, James A. Letter to the Republican voters of the Nineteenth District, Hiram, Ohio, 1873.

————. "National Appropriations and Misappropriations." *North American Review,* 1879. Vol. 128.

——————. "Symposium on Negro Suffrage." *North American Review,* 1879. Vol. 128.

——————. *Review of the Transactions of the Credit Mobilier Company.* Washington, 1873.

——————., in *Messages and Papers of the Presidents, 1789-1897,* James D. Richardson, ed. 10 vol. Washington, 1896-99. VIII, 1-32.

Garfield Papers. New York Public Library.

Garfield Papers. Library of Congress.

Morton Papers. New York Public Library.

Official Bulletin of the Autopsy on the Body of President Garfield, *Medical Record.* New York, 1881. Vol XX, 364.

Official Records, War of the Rebellion. Series I, Vols. 7, 10, 12, 23, 30, 31.

Proceedings of the Republican National Convention. Chicago, 1880.

Sherman Papers. Library of Congress.

Star Route Frauds. Report in House Misc. Doc. No. 38, 48th Cong., lst Sess., Pt. 2.

DIARIES, LETTERS AND PUBLIC ADDRESSES

Blaine, Mrs. James G., *The Letters of Mrs. James G. Blaine,* H.S.B. Beale, ed. 2 vols. New York, 1908.

Curtis, George William, *Orations and Addresses of George William Curtis,* Charles Eliot Norton, ed. 3 vols. New York, 1904.

Garfield, James A., in *Messages and Papers of the Presidents, 1789-1897,* James D. Richardson, ed. 10 vols. Washington, 1896-99. VIII, pp. 1-32.

Hayes, Rutherford B., *The Diary and Letters of Rutherford Burchard Hayes,* Charles R. Williams, ed. 5 vols. Columbus, Ohio, 1922-26.

Shurz, Carl, *Speeches, Correspondence, and Political Papers of Carl Schurz,* Frederic Bancroft, ed. 6 vols. New York, 1913.

GENERAL WORKS

Binkley, Wilfred E. *American Political Parties: Their Natural History.* New York, 1943.

Bowers, Claude G. *The Tragic Era; the Revolution After Lincoln.* New York, 1929.

Coolidge, Mary R. *Chinese Immigration.* New York, 1929.

Ewing, E.A.M. *Presidential Elections from Abraham Lincoln to Franklin D. Roosevelt.* New York, 1940.

Hofstadter, Richard. *The Age of Reform.* New York, 1955.*

Josephson, Matthew. *The Politicos, 1865-1896.* New York, 1938.*

Merrill, H.S. *Bourbon Democracy of the Middle West, 1865-1896.* New York, 1953.

Oberholtzer, E.P. *A History of the United States Since the Civil War.* 5 vols. New York, 1917-37.

Roseboom, E.H. *A History of Presidential Elections.* New York, 1957.

Rothman, D. J. *Politics and Power: The United States Senate, 1869-1901.* New York, 1966.

Schlesinger, Arthur M. *The Rise of the City.* New York, 1933.

Stanwood, Edward. *American Tariff Controversies in the Nineteenth Century.* 2 vols. Boston, 1903.

Woodward, C. Vann. *Origins of the New South, 1877-1913.* New York, 1951.*

BIOGRAPHIES

Balch, W.R. *From the Towpath to the White House.* New York, 1882. This was the most popular of the early biographies of Garfield.

Bundy, J.M. *The Life of James A. Garfield.* New York, 1880. This was the authorized campaign biography by the editor of the *New York Evening Mail.*

Caldwell, R.G. *James A. Garfield: Party Chieftan.* New York, 1931. This is the latest and best biography of Garfield to date. It contains a dated, but good bibliography.

Conwell, Russell H. *The Life, Speeches, and Public Services of James A. Garfield.* Portland, Maine, 1881. This was a memorial biography of Garfield. Highly laudatory, but contains some good information.

Fuller, Corydon E. *Reminiscences of James A. Garfield.* Cincinnati, Ohio, 1887. An important source for the early life of Garfield

Gilmore, J.R. *The Life of James A. Garfield.* New York, 1880. Rather superficial work without much depth or critical appraisal.

Harmon, Joseph. *Garfield, the Lawyer.* New York, 1929. This work deals with Garfield's early career, and Congressional years. Some valuable material.

Hinsdale, B.A., ed. *The Works of James A. Garfield.* 2 vols. Boston, 1882. A very complete compilation of Garfield's speeches and letters. Each document is preceded by an able introduction.

—————. *President Garfield and Education.* Boston, 1882. Discusses Garfield's appreciation of and contributions to American education.

Howe, George F. *Chester A. Arthur: A Quarter Century of Machine Politics.* New York, 1935. While this is the only biography of Arthur, it is scholarly and perceptive. It has been reprinted as part of the American Classics Series (1957) and evaluates Arthur's career critically.

Ridpath, John C. *The Life and Work of James A. Garfield.* New York, 1881. A short, not especially critical work, but with much information of Garfield's early years.

Smith, Theodore C. *The Life and Letters of James Abram Garfield.* 2 vols. New Haven, Conn., 1925. Full and scholarly in its quotations of manuscripts, and especially useful for Garfield's early years. Many of the conclusions on controversial topics require more critical examination.

MEMOIRS AND OTHER BIOGRAPHIES

Barnard, Harry. *Rutherford B. Hayes and His America.* New York, 1954.

Boutwell, George S. *Reminiscences of Sixty Years in Public Affairs,* 2 vols. New York, 1902.

Conkling, Alfred R. *The Life and Letters of Roscoe Conkling, Orator, Statesman, Advocate.* New York, 1889.

Foster, John W. *Diplomatic Memoirs.* 2 vols. Boston, 1909.

Fuess, Claude M. *Carl Schurz, Reformer.* New York, 1902.

Godkin, Edwin L., *Life and Letters of Edwin Lawrence Godkin,* Rollo Ogden, ed. 2 vols. New York, 1907.

Muzzey, D.F. *James G. Blaine: A Political Idol of Other Days.* New York, 1934.

Nevins, Allan. *Grover Cleveland: A Study in Courage.* New York, 1932.

Platt, Thomas C. *The Autobiography of Thomas Collier Platt.* New York, 1910.

Sherman, John. *Recollections of Forty Years in the House, Senate, and Cabinet.* 2 vols. Chicago, 1895.

Sievers, H.J. *Benjamin Harrison: Hoosier Statesman.* New York, 1959.

Wise, John S. *Recollections of Thirteen Presidents.* New York, 1906.

PAMPHLETS

Blaine, James G. *Foreign Policy of the Garfield Administration, Chicago, 1882.*

Brown, Willard. *Civil Service Reform in the New York Custom House.* New York, 1882.

Hurlbert, William H. *Meddling and Muddling, Mr. Blaine's Foreign Policy.* Privately printed in 1884.

Morgan, James. *America's Egypt.* New York, 1884.

Royall, William L. *The President's Relations with Senator Mahone and Repudiation. An Attempt to Subvert the Supreme Court of the United States.* New York, 1882.

Strobel, Edward M. *Mr. Blaine and His Foreign Policy.* Boston, 1884.

The Garfield and Arthur Campaign Songster. Cincinnati, 1880.

POLITICS AND REFORM

Clancy, H. J. *The Presidential Election of 1880.* New York, 1958.

Eaton, Dorman B. *The Independent Movement in New York.* New York, 1880.

Fish, Carl R. *The Civil Service and the Patronage.* New York, 1905.

Ginger, Ray. *Age of Excess.* New York, 1965.*

Glasson, William H. *Federal Military Pensions in the United States.* New York, 1918.

Goldman, Eric F. *Rendevouz With Destiny: A History of Modern American Reform.* New York, 1952.*

Hepburn, A. Barton. *A History of Currency in the United States*. New York, 1924.

Hogenboom, Ari. *Fighting the Spoilsman*. New York, 1960.

Sageser, A.B. *The First Two Decades of the Pendleton Act*. New York, 1935.

Stanwood, Edward. *American Tariff Controversies in the Nineteenth Century*. 2 vols. Boston, 1903.

Taussig, F.W. *The Tariff History of the United States,* New York, 1914.*

Van Riper, P.P. *History of the United States Civil Service*. New York, 1958.

White, Leonard D. *The Republican Era*. New York, 1958.*

INDEX

148

TITLES IN THE OCEANA
PRESIDENTIAL CHRONOLOGY SERIES
Reference books containing
Chronology—Documents—Bibliographical Aids
for each President covered.
Series Editor: **Howard F. Bremer**

GEORGE WASHINGTON*
edited by Howard F. Bremer

JOHN ADAMS*
edited by Howard F. Bremer

JAMES BUCHANAN*
edited by Irving J. Sloan

GROVER CLEVELAND**
edited by Robert I. Vexler

FRANKLIN PIERCE*
edited by Irving J. Sloan

ULYSSES S. GRANT**
edited by Philip R. Moran

MARTIN VAN BUREN**
edited by Irving J. Sloan

THEODORE ROOSEVELT**
edited by Gilbert Black

BENJAMIN HARRISON*
edited by Harry J. Sievers

JAMES MONROE*
edited by Ian Elliot

WOODROW WILSON**
edited by Robert I. Vexler

RUTHERFORD B. HAYES*
edited by Arthur Bishop

ANDREW JACKSON**
edited by Ronald Shaw

JAMES MADISON**
edited by Ian Elliot

HARRY S TRUMAN***
edited by Howard B. Furer

WARREN HARDING**
edited by Philip Moran

DWIGHT D. EISENHOWER***
edited by Robert I. Vexler

JAMES K. POLK*
edited by John J. Farrell

JOHN QUINCY ADAMS*
edited by Kenneth Jones

HARRISON/TYLER***
edited by David A. Durfee

ABRAHAM LINCOLN***
edited by Ian Elliot

GARFIELD/ARTHUR***
edited by Howard B. Furer

Available Soon

WILLIAM McKINLEY
edited by Harry J. Sievers

ANDREW JOHNSON
edited by John N. Dickinson

WILLIAM HOWARD TAFT
edited by Gilbert Black

JOHN F. KENNEDY
edited by Ralph A. Stone

THOMAS JEFFERSON
edited by Arthur Bishop

TAYLOR/FILLMORE
edited by John J. Farrell

CALVIN COOLIDGE
edited by Philip Moran

LYNDON B. JOHNSON
edited by Howard B. Furer

FRANKLIN D. ROOSEVELT
edited by Howard F. Bremer

HERBERT HOOVER
edited by Arnold Rice

*   96 pages, $3.00/B
** 128 pages, $4.00/B
*** 160 pages, $5.00/B